Heroes and Villains of the British Empire

Dedicated to
Lesley Garrod
Or, in the spirit of one character that readers
will meet with in this book,
She-Who-Must-Be-Obeyed.

Heroes and Villains of the British Empire

Their Lives and Legends

Stephen Basdeo

PEN & SWORD
HISTORY

First published in Great Britain in 2020 by
Pen & Sword History
An imprint of
Pen & Sword Books Ltd
Yorkshire – Philadelphia

ISBN 978 1 52674 939 0

Printed and bound by CPI Group (UK) Ltd,
Croydon, CR0 4YY.

Pen & Sword Books Limited incorporates the imprints of Atlas,
Archaeology, Aviation, Discovery, Family History, Fiction, History,
Maritime, Military, Military Classics, Politics, Select, Transport,
True Crime, Air World, Frontline Publishing, Leo Cooper, Remember
When, Seaforth Publishing, The Praetorian Press, Wharncliffe
Local History, Wharncliffe Transport, Wharncliffe True Crime
and White Owl.

For a complete list of Pen & Sword titles please contact

PEN & SWORD BOOKS LIMITED
47 Church Street, Barnsley, South Yorkshire, S70 2AS, England
E-mail: enquiries@pen-and-sword.co.uk
Website: www.pen-and-sword.co.uk

Or

PEN AND SWORD BOOKS
1950 Lawrence Rd, Havertown, PA 19083, USA
E-mail: Uspen-and-sword@casematepublishers.com
Website: www.penandswordbooks.com

Contents

Round the world on your bugles blown!
Where shall the watchful sun,
     England, my England,
Match the master-work you've done,
     England, my own?
When shall he rejoice again
Such a breed of mighty men
As come forward, one to ten,
     To the Song on your bugles blown,
        England –
     Down the years on your bugles blown?
...

Mother of Ships whose might,
     England, my England,
Is the fierce old Sea's delight,
     England, my own,
Chosen daughter of the Lord,
Spouse-in-Chief of the ancient Sword,
There's the menace of the Word
     In the Song on your bugles blown,
        England –
     Out of heaven on your bugles blown!

William Henley, *Pro Rege Nostro* (1900)

'England is never without some little or contemptible war upon her hands.'

George William MacArthur Reynolds (1814–79)

Acknowledgments

I would first like to thank Dr Josh Poklad (Leeds Trinity University) who proof-read this manuscript (before the official proof-reader from Pen and Sword had a look) and offered advice on several parts of the book, pointing out places where further clarification was needed. The book would have been much the poorer without his critical yet friendly eyes reading over the first draft.

As ever, my former supervisors, Professor Paul Hardwick, Professor Rosemary Mitchell, and Dr Alaric Hall deserve a special mention. Although they were not involved in this particular project, without their excellent supervision throughout my PhD in which I developed my skills as a cultural historian, this book would never have been written. They truly are the best supervisors which any aspiring graduate student could hope to study under. I would also like to thank Dr Helen Kingstone: part of the idea for writing this book, as I explain in the second chapter, came from having read her excellent new monograph *Victorian Narratives of the Recent Past: Memory, History, Fiction* (2017), and readers can find out why her work was integral to this book, along with that of J.A. Mangan.

Other academics deserve special thanks here. Professor Alexander Kaufman and Dr Valerie Johnson, although they are not historians of empire, have on many occasions in the past provided me with feedback on my writing in other projects and have helped me to develop my writing skills; and my good friend Dr Mark Truesdale, with whom I have worked on many projects.

Many grateful thanks are also due to Dr Rebecca Nesvet. Since I was a young MA student, she has helped me with many projects I have worked with on Victorian penny bloods and dreadfuls. She is the expert in this area and virtually every piece of academic work I've produced would be poorer without her friendly input. Likewise thanks go to Dr Koenraad Claes and Dr Vanessa Pupavac for having suggested several excellent sources.

To people at my own institution, Richmond American International University (RIASA Leeds), I also say a big thank you: Dr Colin Howley, the programme manager, is one of the best line managers any early career academic could wish to work for, and Dr Lucia Morawska is always ready to provide light relief, and of course Dr Samantha Bracey.

Working at Richmond allowed me the opportunity to teach some gifted students who had many wonderful insights into the topic of imperialism (and the debates in class could sometimes be quite heated). And I want to give a shout out to the students in COMS4100: Connor Vivaldi, Michael Ardourel, Dawson Christina, Sidney Masuka, Trent Innocenti, Sol Griffin, Elliot Ash – I salute you!

My family gets a special mention in all of my books. My parents, Deborah and Joseph Basdeo, who provided much support throughout my education, and my sister Jamila, her husband Andrew, and their children Mya and Alexa deserve a big kiss; Andrew's mother Lesley is sadly no longer with us but hopefully she would have liked the dedication! Likewise my friends, Richard Neesam, Chris Williams, and Sam Dowling – love all three of you!

Also, my cousin Melissa Willock for providing me with the details of my aunt's early life – it's surprising I never asked about this before now! And to Jamie Wheatley, of Premier World Fitness: a friend whom, like one or two of the Victorian schoolmasters featured in this book, tries to get me to appreciate the virtue of fitness but alas!–I'm not always the best pupil.

And to soon-to-be Dr Rachael Gillibrand, the star of Leeds University's Institute of Medieval Studies – we are both fans of Rider Haggard's *She-Who-Must-Be-Obeyed* (Rachael will remember watching with me the dodgy 1980s adaptation of *She* starring Sandahl Bergman in the title role, set in a post-nuclear 'Mad Max' style wasteland where she battles a tutu-wearing giant, a psychic communist, toga-wearing werewolves, and mutants bandaged up like Egyptian mummies – fun times!)

And of course my cat, Robin (or, *He-Who-Must-Be-Obeyed*) – the often moody but loveable little bugger.

Jon Wright and the other wonderful people at Pen and Sword deserve a special mention here too. This is the fourth book I have written for them and I am very grateful to them for taking a chance on me back in

2016 when they contracted me to write *Wat Tyler* (2018). The production staff are always helpful and Laura Hirst deserves a special mention here, who is very understanding of my hasty and panicky last minute proof changes. And thank you to my editor Barnaby Blacker – I am very sorry you had your work cut out with tense changes and misuses of em dashes, semi-colons, and odd sentence constructions. Forgive me!

While in an academic work lengthy notes would be required, this is only a commercial history book, so notes have been kept as brief as possible. Yet I am standing upon the shoulders of some very tall people here and there are numerous historians whose work I have drawn upon to write this book. So, where other historians or literary critics make specific points, I have generally credited them by name in the main body of the text. I urge readers to seek out some of these writers' works that are listed in the bibliography because in the footnotes only references to primary sources have been listed.

Finally, unless otherwise stated, all images in this book are from my personal collection. However, a special note of thanks should go to the Wellcome Library in London, who make all of their images available free of charge. Readers may not know this, but usually researchers have to pay through the nose for the rights to use images in their books when they get them from galleries and libraries (even though, oftentimes, the researcher's taxes fund some of these institutions, which means we're paying twice – but I digress). So thank you, Wellcome Library!

Preface: 'Checking Out Me History'

Out of every ten prefaces, or attempts at introductory matter, to publications as trifling as that which follows, nine of the number may fairly be considered as merely apologetical; or, in other words, they are lowly intercessions with the public for undue mercy and indulgence. That mine should be similar to most others, therefore, is no very great wonder. But still, as most men, when they bespeak favour, endeavour to set forth in goodly array, all the little claims they fancy they may possess for such consideration towards themselves, in this particular also, must I follow the example of my neighbours, and explain, as well as the occasion will allow me, why I venture in the following pages, to intrude on the public notice.

Henry Henderson Barkley, *The Bengalee* (1829)

In concert with Mr Henderson Barkley, I feel that I – a historian of Wat Tyler's Rebellion, Robin Hood, and a bit of nineteenth-century radical history – should explain why I have spent time researching a topic which has little to do with anything I have previously written about. I chose to embark upon this project because, in one small way, my family and I are a living legacy of the British Empire. My father was born in British Guiana (now Guyana), which was Britain's only colony on the South American mainland, in 1957, and my mother is English, born in Durham in 1961. As a history student and one who is very proud of his British and Commonwealth heritage, I wanted to make my own little contribution to the writing on the history of the empire. What follows, therefore, is my 'apologetical' preface.

While many members of the general public today are familiar with the fact that Britain ruled India, owing to movies such as *Viceroy's House* (2017) and *Victoria and Abdul* (2017), fewer people are familiar with the fact that Britain even had a colony on the South American mainland.

One might say it was a 'forgotten' colony; it certainly remains so among British university lecturers, for there are very few histories of the region written by British academics. Yet the encounter between the indigenous Guyanese and English people stretches back to the early modern period. Walter Raleigh was one of the first Englishmen to record his adventures in the region, which was published as *The Discovery of the Large, Rich, and Beautiful Empire of Guiana* (1595). In Guiana, so he thought, the fabled golden city of El Dorado could be found. The country captivated him:

Sir Walter Raleigh (1552–1618) who wrote *The Discovery of the Large, Rich, and Beautiful Empire of Guiana* in 1596.

We passed the most beautiful country that ever mine eyes beheld; and whereas all that we had seen before was nothing but woods, prickles, bushes, and thorns, here we beheld plains of twenty miles in length, the grass short and green, and in divers parts groves of trees by themselves, as if they had been by all the art and labour in the world so made of purpose; and still as we rowed, the deer came down feeding by the water's side as if they had been used to a keeper's call. Upon this river there were great store of fowl, and of many sorts; we saw in it divers sorts of strange fishes, and of marvellous bigness; but for lagartos (alligators and caymans) it exceeded.

It was the Dutch who first established military and economic control over the region in 1600. Formal British rule did not begin until 1796, and

British control over the area was subsequently expanded in 1814 after further territory was ceded to them by the Dutch. Guyana's economy was an agricultural one which depended primarily upon sugar exports. Throughout the period of Dutch rule and during the early period of British rule, slaves from Africa were transported to the region to harvest these and other cash crops. With the end of slavery in 1833, which had been effected in full by 1838, indentured labourers from other parts of the British Empire were transported to Guiana to work in the fields, and many of these workers came from India. My father assumes that it is from India that his ancestors were originally taken as the colony needed indentured labour to work on its plantations during the nineteenth century. While there were some small-scale rebellions which the British government faced in Guyana during the nineteenth century, there was never any revolt on the scale of what the British authorities faced in other parts of the empire, such as India in 1857.

My father vaguely recalls being taught the history of Guiana at school as well as British history. The qualifications which children studied towards were the same as those taught in UK schools. The teaching of British history in Guyanese schools is also attested by the Guyanese poet John Agard, who in *Checking Out Me History* recalls:

> Dem tell me bout Florence Nightingale and she lamp
> and how Robin Hood used to camp
> Dem tell me bout ole King Cole was a merry ole soul
> But dem never tell me bout Mary Seacole.[1]

Agard's poem, written in a West Indian dialect (hence the 'checking out *me* history') expresses conflicted feelings about his own personal identity towards both his heritage as a Guyanese person and his youth and education in a British school system, while my father has never really expressed strong opinions either in favour of or against British rule in Guyana.

In 1966 Guyana received its independence from Britain during the wave of decolonization that occurred in the post-war period although the country remains a member of the Commonwealth of Nations to this day. It was in the 1960s that my father's family decided to emigrate from the recently independent Guyana to the United Kingdom. The process through which a resident of a former colony of the empire might become a naturalized British citizen was easier in those days.[2] While father was studying for his PhD in physics at a university in the north of England – obviously in the days before ridiculously high student fees – he met my mother, who lived in Bowburn, Durham. Mother and father then moved to Leeds where my sister and I were born. Mother was not the only one in our family to have married a person of colour who had emigrated from a former colony to the UK, for my aunt, Claudina, is from Antigua. Her mother arrived in the UK in 1952, found accommodation in Hackney, London, and worked to establish herself. Every year she would send for one of her children; Claudina was the third child to make the journey over with a family friend. In 1970, Claudine married my mum's brother, Raymond, and both of them settled in London's East End where my cousins, Melissa, Louise, and Benjamin were born.

Immigrants from the former empire often faced discrimination in the mid-twentieth century when they came to Britain. It was common to see housing rent advertisements read something along the lines of 'No Blacks, No Dogs, No Irish'. As more immigrants arrived in Britain from India and Pakistan in the late 1960s and 1970s, it was not unusual to see 'Blacks' replaced with 'coloureds' or some other derogatory phrase. There was also the likes of Enoch Powell who said it was 'insane … we that we actually permit unmarried persons to immigrate for the purpose of founding a family with spouses and fiancées whom they have never seen'. There were many journalists in the conservative press at the time, indeed, who criticised the idea of interracial marriage. Yet clearly my mother's family, the Trundleys, held more progressive views.

Throughout history nations have conquered one another and extended their reach and influence over territories. The British were no different in this respect. There is indeed much to criticise about the British Empire. These criticisms have often been highlighted by journalists in the liberal media who have a tendency to attribute all of modern society's racial problems to the empire's legacy. But from my own personal point of view, had the British never assumed control of Guyana, if it had perhaps fallen into the hands of some other European colonizing power, then it is unlikely that my mother and father would ever have met each other,

Government House in Georgetown, Guyana, designed by Joseph Hadfield and completed in 1834. The building now houses the Guyanese Parliament.

which makes it further unlikely that my sister and I would ever have been born. I cannot, indeed, be the only person whose existence today is owed to the fact that Britain once had an empire.

Thus, now I have explained my own Commonwealth connections and my motivations for writing this book, I should say that this is neither a family history nor is it a history of the British Empire as such. Instead, this is a cultural history which tells the story of how British imperialists such as Robert Clive (1725–74), General Gordon (1833–85), and Lord Roberts of Kandahar (1832–1914) were idealised in popular literature during the Victorian period, and transformed into heroes in novels, biographies, and magazines. This is why only a brief overview of British imperial history has been given in the next chapter, to provide a historicised foundation for what ensues. Popular literary works served an important function because academic historians in the Victorian era often eschewed writing histories of their own recent past. They often deemed anything after the Glorious Revolution of 1688 as 'too recent' to constitute 'proper' history. As Helen Kingstone notes, Victorians' memory of the century preceding them and of the rise of their empire was 'diffused and displaced into genres including autobiography, biography, and the novel'. The focus of many of these creative works and biographies was the military hero, who had a special place in late-Victorian popular culture. Men such as Clive were the 'great men' of the empire. The Victorians' attitude to such figures was encapsulated by Thomas Carlyle in *On Heroes and Hero-Worship* (1840) who said that 'the soul of the whole world's history, it may justly be considered, were the history of these'.[3] It was only through popular literature, as Andrew S. Thompson argues, that Victorian readers gained 'an awareness of Britain's imperial past'. Literary works celebrating the glorious and heroic deeds of the men of the empire appeared during what was a very 'jingoistic' era, a word which comes from the music hall song *By Jingo* (1878) which praised the military superiority of the British Empire:

> We don't want to fight; but, by Jingo, if we do,
> We've got the ships, we've got the men,
> We've got the money too.[4]

Red was the colour which marked out British colonies and dominions on world maps, which were a regular sight on the walls of late-Victorian school rooms. Other songs such as *Another Little Patch of Red* (1899) celebrated imperial conquests and the addition of more red-coloured territories to the map of British imperial possessions.[5] In literary works, the men who built the empire were often portrayed in works of fiction as possessing certain abilities which enabled them to serve their country in often inhospitable territories, and spread what imperial ideologues saw as the benefits of the British Empire and civilisation to supposedly 'savage' peoples in far flung corners of the world through the promotion of Commerce, Christianity, and Civilisation – the 'Three Cs' of empire. To promote those values, imperialists were urged to cultivate a unique set of qualities and abilities: athleticism and sporting prowess; a sense of fair play and chivalry; devotion to God and the Christian religion; and a fervent sense of duty and loyalty to the nation and the empire. In other words, these were values of the public schools, institutions which provided the empire with a steady stream of officers and administrators to man the empire.

The original idea for writing this book came from reading the works, not only of Helen Kingstone, but also J.A. Mangan's *The Games Ethic and Imperialism* (1986). Mangan's work was a study of how the above qualities of athleticism, fair play, and patriotism were imparted to youngsters in the public school system. The original idea was to take Mangan's public school ethos, or as he terms it, 'the games ethic', and see how literary portrayals of historical imperialists in the late-Victorian period corresponded to his theory. Yet the scope of this work rapidly expanded, not least because one can hardly talk about the presence of imperial ideology in popular literature without a consideration of what material factors contributed to making literature popular and affordable for readers. The second chapter, therefore, gives a brief history of the growth of the nineteenth-century publishing industry. We then move in the second, third, fourth, and fifth chapters to a discussion of the texts themselves, and an examination of how the imperial heroes were represented. While the majority of sources discussed in these chapters were in fact published during the era of 'new' imperialism (c. 1880–1914), it was important to discuss the longer histories of athleticism, fair play, and patriotism, for none of these ideologies emerged in a vacuum.

It is all well and good to study accounts of the heroes of the empire, but a further aspect of this work which I thought worthy of consideration was anti-heroes of the empire such as outlaws, pirates, and general ne'er-do-wells, whose stories, set in the colonies, competed for popularity with the conventional tales of great men.

And if one discusses popular literature, it seemed I would be doing readers a disservice if I had not given an overview of opposing and critical views of imperialism found in the radical and socialist press; there was after all a rich radical tradition of criticising imperialism in the nineteenth century – the empire did not enjoy unanimous support among Victorians themselves.

We then move into the twentieth century by exploring the various factors which might explain how and why the image of the imperial military hero declined in popular culture.

Key Terms

The words 'empire' and 'imperialism' require some discussion before proceeding. The historian Stephen Howe argues that empire exists when one polity exerts political, economic, and cultural control over another. This may in many cases involve a system of formal rule, as in the British case, when administrators and soldiers were sent out to colonies to rule them. Imperialism is the ideology and actions taken by those in the dominant nation (the 'core') which support and maintain an empire or hegemony over outlying regions (the 'peripheries'). For example, imperialists in the nineteenth century often justified the existence of their empire on the basis that non-British peoples were 'less civilised' and *needed* British rule.

A country need not have a formal empire to be classed as an 'imperialist' nation. The USA in our modern era, for example, can be said to have an imperialist foreign policy because it exerts significant political power over other regions of the world through diplomacy and its military might. Similarly, we can speak also of other forms of imperialism, such as economic imperialism, whereby the hegemony of one particular nation, country, or group of nations (such as 'the West') is maintained over less powerful nations through organisations such as the International Monetary Fund (IMF). We can also envisage imperialism in cultural terms: the culture of one nation or region, through 'products' such as films and music, can be exported to other nations and dominate other cultures. Colonization refers to the large scale movement and settlement of people from the core to the periphery, while colonialism refers to the ideology which justifies colonization.

Chapter 1

At Heaven's Command

But see! to *Britain's* Isle the Squadrons stand,
And leave the sinking Towers, and lessening Land,
The Royal Bark bounds o'er the floating Plain,
Breaks thro' the Billows, and divides the Main,
O'er the vast Deep, Great Monarch, dart thine Eyes,
A wat'ry Prospect bounded by the Skies:
Ten thousand Vessels, from ten thousand Shores,
Bring Gums and Gold, and either India's Stores:
Behold the Tributes hastening to thy Throne,
And see the wide Horizon all thy own.
Thomas Tickell, The Royal Progress (1714)

From pole to pole she hears her acts resound,
And rules an empire by no ocean bound;
Knows her ships anchor'd, and her sails unfurl'd,
In other Indies and a second world.
Long shall *Britannia* (that must be her name)
Be first in conquest, and preside in fame.
Matthew Prior, Solomon (1718)

When Britain first, at Heaven's command
Arose from out the azure main;
This was the charter of the land,
And guardian angels sang this strain:
"Rule, Britannia! Britannia rule the waves:
"Britons never will be slaves."
Thomas Arne, Rule Britannia (1740)

In 1497, Britain 'arose from out the azure main', in the words of the popular patriotic song *Rule Britannia*. In that year, King Henry VII of England (r. 1485–1509), having witnessed the rise of the Spanish Empire and the Portuguese Empire, commissioned a Venetian named John Cabot (c. 1450–1500) to find a trade route to Asia through the North Atlantic. Cabot landed at what is now Newfoundland, Canada.[6] While there, he encountered some of the indigenous people of the region, the Inuit, and brought one of them back to present to his sponsor, the king. Cabot was then commissioned for a second voyage but very little is known as to whether this first attempt to find the famed Northwest Passage was successful. While no colony was established as a result of Cabot's voyages, it did mark a desire on the part of some English rulers to begin exploring the world.

Cabot and his son Sebastien were held in high esteem by historians and historical fiction writers in the Victorian period. Their early adventures kick-started British imperial expansion, 'and no list of its "builders"

King Henry VII who commissioned an exploratory trade route and whom, several Victorian popular histories of the British Empire maintained, was responsible for first setting Britain on the path to imperial greatness.

would be complete without their names'.[7] J.E. Wetherell expressed similar sentiments in 1928:

John Cabot died in 1499 or 1500, a broken-hearted man. He thought his career was a failure, but all the world now knows it was a glorious success. The riches of the East were not to be his, but he had discovered a land which one day was to become greater and richer than his wildest dreams.[8]

There were very few book-length biographies or novels celebrating John Cabot's career, perhaps owing to the general scarcity of sources on his life. Cabot was essentially a footnote in the history of the empire, but as the comments above illustrate, he was an important footnote and his achievements always deserved an honourable mention in the annals of the British Empire.

Looking back over the history of British imperialism, it seems inconceivable that England, a nation located on a small windy rainy island on the edge of Europe, which before the early modern period was a backwater, managed to extend its influence over the entire globe and emerge as the supreme world power by the 1800s. The common saying was that 'the sun never sets on the British Empire'. Britain's rise to world power status seems all the more improbable when, for some time after Cabot's voyages, English rulers showed little interest in imperial endeavours. While Henry VII commissioned Cabot's voyage, his son, Henry VIII (r. 1509–47), showed little interest in the world beyond domestic and European politics and, of course, was a rather bad husband to his many wives.

Attitudes started to change during the reign of Queen Elizabeth I (r. 1558–1603), a young protestant queen whose kingdom challenged the might of the Spanish Empire, the superpower of the day. John Dee in *General and Rare Memorials* (1577) argued that the English nation ought to found an empire to rival that of Spain's. It would be incumbent on the English government to maintain a strong navy, the cost of which should be borne by the nation. He even came up with a brand new name for this empire: this was to be a 'British Empire'.[9] Dee's statement marked the first use of the term in history. It will be noticed that Dee, although he was writing to fellow English people, conflated the idea of an English Empire with that of a British Empire, even though the passage of the Act of Union with Scotland in 1707 was a long way off.

Dee's remarks on the need for a strong naval fleet were all the more urgent because the English navy had been left to languish under Henry VIII. In 1558, England had only twenty-six ships in its fleet, and tensions with Spain were brewing. While a strong navy was needed for defence, England was not a rich nation. So, in 1562, Elizabeth I authorised the privateers – state-sanctioned pirates to all intents and purposes – John Hawkins (1532–95) and Francis Drake (1563–96) to begin raiding Spanish slaving ships and stealing gold. This was still very much a reaction to European politics rather than a statement of imperial ambitions. Tensions with Spain had spilled over into outright war by 1585, so England sought to break into this very lucrative though reprehensible trade and make life difficult for the Spanish.

Some attempts to establish overseas colonies in the Elizabethan period were made by Humphrey Gilbert (1539–83) and Walter Raleigh

Queen Elizabeth I, who granted a charter to The Governor and Company of Merchants of London Trading into the East Indies, marking the beginning of an Anglo-Indian trading relationship which would culminate in the rise of an empire.

but the settlements were often badly planned. Raleigh's Roanoke Colony in present-day North Carolina failed because the colonists ran out of supplies. A colony established in Guiana in 1604 lasted only two years for similar reasons. One of the only long-lasting and major developments in the history of the British Empire during Elizabeth's reign occurred in the year 1600 when the queen granted a Royal Charter to a joint-stock company named The Governor and Company of Merchants of London Trading into the East

The Elizabethan writer John Dee who wrote *General and Rare Memorials* (1577) which is the first literary work to have used the term 'British Empire'.

Indies (hereafter called 'the East India Company'). The charter gave the company a monopoly over English trade with Asia, meaning that no other English company could transact business there without royal permission. This was not a state-sponsored enterprise but one spearheaded by wealthy merchants and aristocrats. During the next two centuries, the Company's trade with China and the various kingdoms and states that made up the Indian Mughal Empire flourished. Eventually the Company established small trading outposts in India known as 'factories' which were fortified trading settlements.

English joint stock companies also established their presence in the Americas ('joint stock' means that multiple individuals share – via 'shares' – the ownership of the company 'stock', and these individuals are free, if they desire, to sell their ownership of company stock to others on a stock exchange). Early modern trading companies did more to spread England's power across the globe than any king, queen, or statesman. Trade was vitally important to the empire. A verse from *Rule Britannia* which is rarely sung today emphasised the importance of trade to the growing empire:

To thee belongs the rural reign;
Thy cities shall with commerce shine;
And thine shall be the — shall be the subject main;
And ev'ry shore it circles, thine.
Rule Britannia, &c.[10]

(The importance of trade during the eighteenth century was one of the reasons why writers condemned pirates, decrying their 'profession' as being 'so destructive to the navigation of the trading world').[11]

Through the agency of these early corporations, settlements were established in the Americas. Jamestown was founded in Virginia in 1607 by the Virginia Company of London and, in spite of a few adversities, the colony thrived. Even the puritan Pilgrims, who landed at what is now Plymouth, Massachusetts in 1620 to escape religious persecution, first had to persuade investors to fund their journey and provide them with capital to buy tools and provisions for the colony to thrive. The journey to the Americas was not an easy one to make and the fledgling colonies might fail meaning that the companies could run into financial difficulties. When the Virginia Company ran into financial difficulties in 1624, its total debt was £9,000 (which, as a proportion of Britain's wealth at the time, translates into perhaps £400 million today) and it struggled to attract new investment. As sometimes happens nowadays when corporations threaten to go bust, the government stepped in; so it was with the Virginia Company that the state stepped in and decided that Virginia would thereafter be run as a Crown Colony.

Imperial endeavours generated a response in popular culture even at this point as authors and poets celebrated the establishment of the American colonies. Michael Drayton's *To the Virginian Voyage* (1606), for example, opened with the following laudatory lines:

You brave Heroique Minds,
Worthy your countries name,
That honour still pursue,
Goe, and subdue,
Whilst loyt'ring Hinds
Lurke here at home, with shame.[12]

This image entitled *Deputies from the Four Corners of the Earth Pay Homage to the Goddess Britannia* was the frontispiece of *The Britannic Magazine* for the Year 1793. It encapsulates the eighteenth-century British Empire's view of itself: its greatness was due to trade.

Yet the public reaction to the establishment of overseas colonies was by no means unanimously positive. An ambivalent attitude to the emerging empire is found in John Fletcher's *Bonduca* (1613), a play which tells the story of the ancient British warrior queen Boudicca who led a fight for independence against the imperialist Roman Empire. The Britons resist the Roman army's advances because they fear it will lead to a loss of their culture, identity, and sense of history, as revealed in the prayer which Bonduca offers to the British gods before the final battle:

> *Bond*: ye powerful gods of Britain, hear our prayers;
> Hear us, ye great revengers; and this day
> Take pity from our swords, doubt from our valours;
> Double the sad remembrance of our wrongs
> In every breast; the vengeance due to those
> Make infinite and endless! On our pikes
> This day pale Terror sit, horrors and ruins
> Upon our executions; claps of thunder
> Hang on our armed carts; and 'fore our troops
> Despair and Death; Shame beyond these attend 'em!
> Rise from the dust, ye relics of the dead,
> Whose noble deeds our holy Druids sing;
> Oh, rise, ye valiant bones! Let not base earth
> Oppress your honours, whilst the pride of Rome
> Treads on your stocks, and wipes out all your stories![13]

Rome represents the fledgling English Empire and the Britons represent the Native American Algonquins. The clash between the Britons and the Romans mirrors the violent encounters between English colonisers and the Native Americans. The Britons fight in a manner that resembles Native Americans by disguising themselves and 'blending in' with the landscape. The similarity of the language which Fletcher used to describe the Britons matches contemporary descriptions of Native Americans. Yet he has no easy answers; the Britons in the play will inevitably succumb to foreign domination. It made Fletcher uneasy: even though English colonisers at this early period only wanted to settle, farm, and make a life for themselves in the New World, and to trade with the indigenous inhabitants of the Americas, he foresaw the end-point of this process.

England and Scotland were still two separate countries when Beaumont and Fletcher were writing. The countries shared one monarch, James I of England and VI of Scotland, under the Union of Crowns. But there were two separate parliaments. While England's empire was increasing in size and economic importance, the Scottish government decided that it too would attempt to establish a colony overseas. The location chosen for the country's first overseas colony was the Gulf of Darién in Panama, and the settlement would be named New Caledonia. To facilitate this venture a joint stock company was formed, called the Company of Scotland, into which rich merchants could invest money. Investors came from both Scotland and England and the company raised over £400,000. So early in 1698, five ships set sail and made landfall in Panama in November of that year. The venture was a complete disaster. Poor planning and lack of provisions meant that the colonists succumbed easily to disease. News of the scheme's failure had not reached Britain before the second expedition of 1,000 people had set off. Besides disease, the second set of adventurers had a new foe with which to contend: the Spanish Empire. The Spanish besieged the new colony for over a month, which saw many of the colonists succumb to disease and starvation. Yet the poor folks holed up in Panama could expect no help from England: King William III instructed his English colonies in North America not to send any aid to Panama for fear of further inflaming tensions with Spain. After the Spanish siege was lifted, the remaining survivors decided to travel back to England, although many died on the way back from fever. Afterwards, the Kingdom of Scotland's parlous financial state was a great encouragement to many of the Scottish elites when it came to supporting the Act of Union with England (1707), as it would mean easy access to English finance for the more affluent among them. The deal was made sweeter because Darién shareholders, under the terms of the union, were to be reimbursed for their losses with interest. When the shareholders were repaid, they formed a new Scottish banking company which eventually became the Royal Bank of Scotland.

Yet the view taken by many Scots in the eighteenth century was that the Scottish people had been bribed into uniting with England, a sentiment still popular in 1791, as revealed in Robert Burns's *Such a Parcel of Rogues in a Nation* which excoriates the Scottish ruling class for agreeing to it:

The English steel we could disdain,
Secure in valour's station;
But English gold has been our bane –
Such a parcel of rogues in a nation!

O would, ere I had seen the day
That Treason thus could sell us,
My auld grey head had lien in clay,
Wi' Bruce and loyal Wallace!
But pith and power, till my last hour,
I'll mak this declaration;
We're bought and sold for English gold –
Such a parcel of rogues in a nation!

Nevertheless, after 1707, England's empire was no longer its own: it was now a truly *British* Empire.

The Caribbean Islands proved to be a lucrative source of income for many British merchants who established plantations in the region. The indigenous people were a formidable adversary for the English settlers in the early years of West Indian colonisation. The first settlement, at St. Lucia, was completely destroyed by the Caribs in 1605 and it was not until seven years later that the next Caribbean colony was founded at Bermuda. Further islands were added to Britain's growing empire, often as a result of various wars against the Spanish, French, and Dutch throughout the seventeenth century. Britain acquired Antigua in 1632 and Barbados in 1655. The islands had little mineral wealth but coffee, sugar, and tobacco thrived on the plantations. The first labourers to arrive in these colonies were indentured labourers, many of whom were white Europeans and had a clearly defined term of service. However, many of them could not stand the climate and the mortality rates were high. Plantation owners began importing African slaves purchased from Dutch slave traders because, they reasoned, people from warmer climates would be able to carry out back-breaking work in the blazing sun much better than their white counterparts. The slaves were brought from Africa, packed inhumanely into ships, and sent to the American and West Indian plantations.

Captain Cook's first encounter with the people of Australia. This illustration is taken from an Edwardian children's book. Cook stands proud and erect while the natives, in a deferential pose, seemed awed by him. This would have been intentional on the illustrator's part; when the book was published in the early 1900s, the 'civilising mission' was in full swing; intellectuals, and many in society-at-large, assumed that the British 'race' occupied a place at the top of the racial hierarchy.

Conservative estimates by historians put the number of slaves transported from Africa at a staggering 12.5 million, with Great Britain alone responsible for the transportation of 3.25 million. Slaves were subject to torture and mutilation, being burned or whipped in public if they committed even minor offences against their masters. The economy of these resource-rich islands, as well as the economies of the British colonies on the American mainland, became heavily dependent on slavery, which continued in the Americas into the mid-nineteenth century.

Slavery became illegal in England as a result of a ruling in the Somerset Case of 1772. A slave named James Somerset had been the 'property' of his master, Charles Stewart, a customs officer in Boston, Massachusetts. Stewart brought Somerset to England with him but once in England Somerset escaped. He remained at large but was eventually recaptured after two years and immediately placed on a ship bound for Jamaica. Fortunately for Somerset, one of the major anti-slavery campaigners at the time, Granville Sharpe (1735–1813), convinced the Chief Justice Lord Mansfield (1705–93), to serve a writ of *habeas corpus* on the captain of the vessel. After much legal wrangling, Somerset appeared before the courts. His counsel argued that, although slavery was legal in the colonies, in England, English common law applied and in this country it was illegal for any man to be enslaved. Lord Mansfield agreed, saying that 'no master ever was allowed [in England] to take a slave by force to be sold abroad because he deserted from his service, therefore the man must be discharged'.[14] Famous authors and poets added their voices to the public debate over slavery, as William Cowper did in *The Task* (1785):

> We have no slaves at home – Then why abroad?
> And they themselves, once ferried o'er the wave
> That parts us, are emancipate and loos'd.
> Slaves cannot breathe in England; if their lungs
> Receive our air, that moment they are free.
> They touch our country, and their shackles fall.
> That's noble, and bespeaks a nation proud.
> And jealous of the blessing. Spread it then,
> And let it circulate through every vein.[15]

Abolition of slavery throughout the empire took much longer, although since its abolition British efforts in opposing slavery have become a source of national pride especially among politicians. Victorian historians likewise regarded abolition as one of the nation's greatest humanitarian achievements. This attitude has largely persisted in popular culture. As recently as 2007, there was the bicentennial commemoration of the Abolition of the Slave Trade Act (1807) and even a movie, *Amazing Grace* (2007), was released which was a biopic of the anti-slavery campaigner William Wilberforce (1759–1833). The film was pure hagiography. It marginalised the role of black abolitionist campaigners such as Olaudah Equiano (1745–97) and the slaves themselves. It elevated Wilberforce to such wonderful heights by depicting him as a man who almost singlehandedly stopped the slave trade. Such a pretty picture, indeed, is painted of Wilberforce in that movie that one would never have guessed that, to citizens at home, he was not so saintly. He rarely voted against the government who at this point were paranoid that the French Revolution would spread to Britain. Wilberforce therefore gave his support to a number of repressive measures such as the Habeas Corpus Suspension

Act (1794), which allowed the government to imprison people without a trial, and lent his support to other acts which curbed British citizens' freedom of speech and assembly. He was not so saintly as some would have us believe. It might justifiably be said that in Wilberforce we have the first prototype of Dickens's Mrs Jellyby who cared much for those in far off places, whose philanthropic efforts assuaged her 'Christian' conscience, but ignored the plight of people in her own backyard.

A medallion designed by Josiah Wedgwood to promote the anti-slavery cause. With thanks to the Wellcome Library.

Wilberforce and his fellow campaigners' efforts ensured the abolition of the slave trade but slavery itself was not abolished until the passage of the Emancipation Act (1833). This Act freed the slaves but only gave financial compensation to the slave owners. While lauded as a humanitarian achievement, a more cynical reading of slavery's abolition came from the Marxist historian Eric Williams (1911–81), who argued that slavery – in the British Empire, the USA, and other European empires – was only abolished once it had become unnecessary and unprofitable. Society had progressed, in Williams's view, from a slave-owning society to a bourgeois industrial-capitalist society. Besides, it was cheaper for capitalists to pay low wages to workers rather than have to maintain a population of slaves. With due respect to Professor Williams, the truth of the matter is that philanthropists certainly played a role in ensuring slavery's abolition in the British Empire, but it was indeed becoming increasingly unnecessary due to the technological advancements of the industrial revolution.

While abolitionists were attempting to convince people to support their cause in the late eighteenth century, tensions were brewing in the Thirteen American Colonies. The colonists felt they should not be forced to pay taxes imposed upon them which had been passed by a parliament in Britain rather than their own colonial assemblies. The colonists responded by boycotting British goods and refusing to pay import duties on goods such as tea. In 1773, angry citizens in Boston, Massachusetts, famously dumped boxes of tea in the harbour, an event now known as the Boston Tea Party. There was also a lesser known 'tea party' which occurred for the same reasons at Yorktown, Virginia, in 1774. Some of the other measures which annoyed the colonists were the so-called Quartering Acts, which required the colonists to fund and provide lodgings, sometimes in their own homes, for British soldiers stationed there. The British government certainly did not make any kind of reconciliation with the inhabitants of the colonies easy. The first Continental Congress was convened in 1774 to draw up a list of grievances to send to the British government back in London but the colonists' demands fell on deaf ears. Tensions with the Americans reached

Frontispiece to Olaudah Equiano's autobiography. With thanks to the Wellcome Library.

boiling point and spilled over into an outright war for independence which lasted from 1776 to 1783. The result of the war is well known: with the help of France, Britain's historic enemy and rival superpower, the Thirteen Colonies won their independence and formed themselves into the United States of America.

It seemed as though Britain's rise to the status of a great imperial power might be nipped in the bud. A popular song in America during the 1780s entitled *Taxation in America* lauded George Washington's victory over the British and proclaimed 'Britain's fading glory'.[16] Yet Britain's 'glory' did anything but fade: as the nation lost its grip over its American colonies, it gained a foothold in Australia due to the 'discoveries' of Captain James Cook. The existence of a great *Terra Australis Incognita* (unknown southern land) was believed in as far back as Ancient Greek and Roman times, and explorers associated with the Dutch East India Company were the first Europeans to meet some of the indigenous people and chart the western coast of Australia and parts of what is now

The leading men of the American Revolution signing the Declaration of Independence on 4 July 4, 1776. Image supplied with thanks to the Wellcome Library.

New Zealand. It was not until Cook was commissioned by the British government to discover more of this great unknown land that the eastern part of Australia was mapped out, along with the entire coast of New Zealand. While officially Cook's voyage was supposed to be one solely of exploration and not colonisation, one of his secret orders from the British government was that he should,

> with the consent of the natives, take possession of convenient situations in the country in the name of the King of Great Britain: or, if you find the country uninhabited take possession for his Majesty by setting up proper marks and inscriptions, as first discoverers and possessors.[17]

Cook set out on the *Endeavour* in 1768 and reached the southern coast of Australia in 1770. He charted the eastern coast of the continent and named the region New South Wales. The settlement of Australia soon followed when the authorities in Britain decided to build a penal colony

A watercolour in the 'Company Style' by Ghulam Ali Khan, Old Mughal minaret near Delhi. Image supplied with thanks to the Wellcome Library.

at Botany Bay, and on 18 January 1788 the first convict ship arrived. Botany Bay was considered to be an unsuitable place to establish a colony due to its swamps, so the site for the penal colony was quickly relocated to Port Jackson, in what is now Sydney. While some free men and woman accompanied the first fleet to New South Wales, it remained predominantly a penal colony until 1793 when the first free settlers arrived. After this, a number of prosperous settlements developed in tandem with the penal colonies.

Nevertheless, the American Revolution certainly marked a turning point: some historians have claimed that there were two British Empires: the first existed from the pioneering trading adventures of the East India Company in the seventeenth century to the loss of the American colonies; the second is considered to have lasted from the American War of Independence onwards till the twentieth century.[18]

In the meantime the East India Company extended its foothold in India. After the death of the Mughal Emperor Aurangzeb in 1707 the French and English companies vied for influence over his weak successors and the semi-independent princely states. The two companies made uneasy alliances with local rulers but when hostilities broke out between France and Britain in 1756 – the beginning of the Seven Years' War which lasted until 1763 – the companies involved themselves in various feuds between local Indian rulers with the aim of securing a commercial advantage over the other. France was allied with the Nawab of Bengal, Siraj ud-Daulah (1733–57) but their campaigns against the British forces were ultimately unsuccessful. As a result of a decisive victory at the Battle of Plassey, led by Robert Clive, the British East India Company annexed the Bengal region. Siraj ud-Daulah was deposed and a Company puppet, Mir Jafar (1691–1765), was installed to rule over the region. Two years after the end of the Seven Years' War, the Mughal Emperor, Shah Alam II (1728–1806), granted the East India Company the *diwani* of Bengal which allowed the Company to raise taxes in that region. The stage was thus set for the East India Company's transition from a mere commercial enterprise into a political power.

The British government was often reluctant to intervene in Company affairs, but nevertheless made its first major intervention in 1773 with the passage of the Regulating Acts. These Acts established a supreme council and Supreme Court to govern the newly-acquired territory. Warren Hastings (1732–1818), governor of Fort St William and head of this Supreme Council took a pragmatic approach to governing the region. Hastings was a great admirer of Indian culture and threw his full support behind the establishment of the Bengal Asiatick Society in 1784, with the aim of increasing British people's knowledge of India's history and culture. The establishment of this society, as well as his sponsorship of the first English translation of the *Bhagavad Gita* in 1785, stemmed from a real love of Indian culture. He is once supposed to have said, 'I love India a little more than my own country.' While many Indians at this period rightly objected to Company rule – evident by the many wars which the Company fought against smaller Indian kingdoms and principalities – we should not underestimate the often cordial relations between the British and Indians in towns such as Calcutta. Phebe Gibbes in *Hartly House, Calcutta* (1789), a novel inspired by letters sent to her from her brother in the Company's employ, relates how both Indians and British people attended the races at Calcutta and mingled together socially.

A European Residence in Madras, India. (*Public Domain image, with thanks to the British Library* (*WD1264300*))

Other people of British descent in India 'went native', like Colonel James Achilles Kirkpatrick (1764–1805). Born in Madras to English parents, he was fluent in Hindustani, Urdu, and Tamil. He converted to Islam, wore Mughal-style clothing, and married Khair-un-Nissa, grand-daughter of the Nawab of Hyderabad. During the same period, in high art there was a fusion of British and Indian styles of painting, now named 'Company Style'. It favoured watercolours over gouache, and its practitioners, mainly Indians, were commissioned by Company employees to depict scenes of Indian life, its people, and its animal and plant life. As an admirer of Indian culture, Hastings advocated only minimal interference in Indians' way of life. After all, the East India Company was still a business so there was little point in annoying the inhabitants who produced the Company's wealth.

It was not only the Company directors who got rich; its foot soldiers did too, accumulating wealth through the seizing of 'prize money' (loot) as a result of fresh conquests. Literary works depicted India as a land of opportunity; serving the Company and acquiring wealth was a means by which English soldiers from relatively humble backgrounds might rise through society's rank, outshining the splendour of even the richest members of the nobility. On their return to Britain these men were branded 'nabobs', a pejorative contraction of 'Nawab', applied to company officials who not only enriched themselves and flaunted their wealth back in Britain much like a Nawab would have done (there is speculation from some modern linguists that our insult 'nob' comes from a contraction of 'nabob'). This is the description which Walter Scott gave of a returning nabob in *The Surgeon's Daughter* (1827):

> It was understood he had served the Honourable East India Company – that wonderful company of merchants, who may indeed, with the strictest propriety, be termed princes. It was about the middle of the eighteenth century, and the directors in Leadenhall Street were silently laying the foundation of that immense empire, which afterwards rose like an exhalation, and now astonishes Europe, as well as Asia, with its formidable extent, and stupendous strength. Britain had now begun to lend a wondering ear to the account of battles

Amidst the decline of the Mughal Empire and the rise of the Company Raj, Tipu Sultan sought to build an alliance of Indian princely states to drive the British out of the subcontinent during the Napoleonic Wars. He was ultimately defeated, however, and his defeat was largely accomplished under the command of an emerging military star: Arthur Wellesley, later appointed as the the Duke of Wellington.

fought, and cities won, in the East; and was surprised by the return of individuals who had left their native country as adventurers, but now reappeared there surrounded by Oriental wealth and Oriental luxury, which dimmed even the splendour of the most wealthy of the British nobility … He spoke, indeed, of making investments, and, as a mere matter of fancy … a few white faces never failed to strike terror into these black rascals; and then, not to mention the good things that were going at the storming of a Pettah, or the plundering of a Pagoda, most of these tawny dogs carried so much treasure about their persons, that a won battle was equal to a mine of gold to the victors.[19]

Scott could have been describing any English nabob. Clive originally entered the Company as a writer before going on to serve in its army. His army service made him immensely rich, having amassed a fortune of over £300,000. Scott's description of a nabob can be taken as representative of the general public feeling towards them back in Britain: they were not much liked. Anyone who reads *The Surgeon's Daughter* will know that Middlemas turns very bad: while in India, at the behest of his mistress Adela Montreville, he lures his childhood sweetheart Menie out to India, to try to sell her to Tipu Sahib for use in his own zenana. Luckily for Menie, another Company officer, the kind-hearted surgeon Adam Hartley, rescues her from being given over to Tipu with the help of Hyder Ali. The latter then punishes Richard by having one of his elephants trample him to death.

Although its officials disdained government interference in its affairs, the Company was increasingly reliant on Westminster for financial and military support. In 1784 parliament passed the India Act which created the office of Secretary of State for India and established the office of Governor-General of India. General Cornwallis was appointed as Governor-General, a position he kept until 1797, although Hastings is often considered the first *de facto* holder of the office. The next Governor-General after Cornwallis was the Marquess of Wellesley (1760–1842), the famous Duke of Wellington's brother (1769–1852). Wellesley's brother faced down a serious revolt against Company rule from Tipu Sultan in 1799. During the Napoleonic Wars, Sultan, who controlled a vast swathe of territory in southern India, attempted to build an alliance of the independent princely states to drive the Company out of India. To accomplish this objective he sought French help, which Napoleon was only too willing to give. One of the reasons for Napoleon's invasion of Egypt was that he wanted to establish a bridge in the Middle East which would give his army easy access to India via the Red Sea and challenge British power in the subcontinent. Sultan's revolt was ultimately unsuccessful however, and he was killed at Seringapatam in the same year. Over the next half century, the East India Company fought further wars and expanded its borders into Burma, Nepal, and the north-western regions bordering Afghanistan, while the conclusion of the Mahratta Wars in Britain's favour in 1818 saw the central part of the subcontinent brought under British rule.

While Company officials took a pragmatic approach to ruling India and resisted attempts by missionaries to meddle with Indian customs, evangelical ideologues at home were becoming more influential in government: the age of the 'do-gooders' had arrived. They had a mission: men such as Wilberforce were advocating for the Christianisation of India, and the subcontinent became their laboratory for testing out liberal theories of government for what they presumed would be for the benefit of all Indians. Another influential thinker at this point was James Mill, whose book *The History of British India* (1817) earned him a bureaucrat's job at India House in London. Mill never visited India but was nevertheless looked upon as an authority on Indian affairs. His history was a 'critical' or 'judging' history, in which he denounced Hindu civilisation as backward. What was needed, so some of his contemporaries thought, was to 'civilise' the subcontinent and remake it in England's image. Thomas Babington Macaulay's comments are representative of this new mindset:

We must at present do our best to form a class who may be interpreters between us and the millions whom we govern; a class of persons, Indian in blood and colour, but English in taste, in opinions, in morals, and in intellect. To that class we may leave it to refine the vernacular dialects of the country, to enrich those dialects with terms of science borrowed from the Western nomenclature, and to render them by degrees fit vehicles for conveying knowledge to the great mass of the population.

From the 1820s onwards, some civil servants, inspired by Bentinck and Macauley's words, truly believed that India needed to be remade in Britain's image. Reforms began to be introduced into India: English became the language of the law courts, and where English administrators felt that certain Indian customs should be outlawed, they did so. This was notably the case with William Bentinck's crusade against *sati*: the self-immolation of Hindu widows on their dead husband's funeral pyres (the practice is often called 'suttee' in Victorian literature). Phebe Gibbs's female protagonist in *Hartly House, Calcutta* in the 1780s – when the Company was lukewarm towards missionaries and men like Hastings had respect for Indian culture – looked upon this rite as a noble and heroic deed, the ultimate manifestation of a woman's love for her husband. Yet to Bentinck and other reformers in the 1820s it was simply evidence of a backward culture. Although the practice was performed rarely by Bentinck's time, a great fuss was made in the press about it. Concern over it even filtered through into popular fiction. Agnes Strickland's *Candava; or, The Last Suttee* (1849) sees a detachment of East India Cavalrymen heroically ride in to a *sati* ceremony to save the Hindu widow Candava, who is moments away from being burnt alive:

Ellen Mortlake, pale and sick with horror, clung to her brother's arm for support, as she gasped out, "Is there no means of preventing this frightful tragedy?"

"It can be prevented and it shall," [Henry Moore] replied, "Lord William Bentinck has abolished Suttee."

[…]

A detachment of British cavalry now dashed through the crowd, with drawn sabres, and Henry Moore, who had outstripped them in all his energetic efforts to prevent the consummation of the sacrifice, darted forward, and struck the torch out of the hand of the obdurate Brahmin, who was in the very act of igniting the fatal combustibles. Then the young officer by whom the brigade was commanded leapt from his horse, sprang upon the pile, and with one stroke of his sabre severed the unhallowed bonds which united the living and the dead, and, raising Candava in his arms, carried her off triumphantly, amidst the shouts of his countrymen and the yells of the disappointed natives, who assailed the gallant soldier with missives in all directions.

"Hold!" he exclaimed, with equal courage and temper, "your resistance is illegal. The British Government has abolished Suttee for ever, and it will be at the peril of life and property if that abomination is ever again attempted in British India."

The widow remains ever grateful to her British saviours. The message here, as in so many such novels which began to be published around the middle of the century, was clear: Indians needed saving from themselves.[20]

Further annexations followed and the Company's last major campaign occurred in 1849 when, as a result of a war against the Sikh Empire, the Punjab came under Company rule. Its progress seemed unstoppable. Yet, if the American Revolution was the first major earthquake felt by the British ruling elite, the next major shock was the Indian Mutiny of 1857, or, as some Indian nationalist historians have it, the War of Indian Independence. India was not a colony settled by the British in the way that America was. It was later boasted that Britain held India

Edward Armitage's *Retribution* (1858). In this painting, the goddess Britannia holds a Bengal Tiger, which represents India, by the neck, ready to plunge her sword into the animal in revenge for the slaying of British women and children during the Indian Mutiny (1857–58). The painting was popular with the gallery-going public and it was reproduced on several occasions in various literary and artistic review periodical. The version reproduced here was reprinted in the first volume of *The Portfolio* in 1870. The original is now in Leeds Art Gallery.

with less than a thousand civil servants. Most of the British-Indian army was composed of Indian Sepoy soldiers under the command of British officers. Empires always require a certain degree of collaboration and the British Empire was no different in this respect; Indians of all religions – Sikhs, Muslims, and Hindus – had served in the Company's army since the eighteenth century. Tensions between Indian soldiers and the Company flared up however, because a rumour spread through the Sepoy ranks which alleged that the bullets for their new Enfield Rifle was laced with pig and cow fat. In an age when soldiers had to bite the outer covering of the cartridge before loading it into the rifle, this meant that both Muslim and Hindu soldiers would be ingesting something which their religions deemed to be unclean: the former viewed the pig as an unclean animal while the latter held the cow to be sacred. Matters came to a head when Sepoys refused to attend rifle drills at Berhampore, while over at Barrackpore, a soldier named Mangal Pandey wounded two British officers in protest. Pandey was hanged but the revolt spread like wildfire. From a mere mutiny of soldiers it grew into a proto-nationalist rebellion. One of the rebels' grievances was exactly what the Company had feared: the attempted Christianisation of India by missionaries. The rebels wanted nothing short of the end of Company rule in India. As their figurehead they chose Bahadur Shah II (1775–1862), who was the nominal ruler of the now almost defunct Mughal Empire. Atrocities were committed by both sides. The rebels besieged Cawnpore in which there was a number of British men, women, and children. Having virtually starved the British out, the rebel leaders agreed to allow the remaining citizens safe passage out of the town to take boats up river to safety. However, as the British made their way onto the boats, the rebels broke their pledge and began firing at them. It truly was a massacre, as the personal account of W.J. Shepherd reveals:

> When the males had all been put to the sword, the order to cease firing was given by the cavalry, and the poor women and children that survived were brought out of the river and collected on the bank. Many of them were wounded with bullets and sword cuts; their dresses were wet and full of mud and blood; they were ordered to give up whatever valuables they might have hid upon their persons.[21]

On the other hand, the British were just as savage in their treatment of Indian civilians when they gained the upper hand. As Alex Tickell notes that in their retribution, British soldiers 'remembered' the colonial dead by embarking on a frenzied bout of 'intoxication, plunder and rapine' through Cawnpore's Indian quarter – a practice that British soldiers would repeat in other cities retaken from the rebels.

After the revolt, the British public wanted vengeance, a desire expressed by a variety of artists, journalists, and novelists. Edward Armitage's *Retribution* (1858) is a case in point: the figure of a muscular goddess Britannia holds a Bengal tiger – representing India – by its neck, ready to plunge her sword into its throat for having killed a British woman and a child. Charles Dickens (1812–70) added his voice to the debate:[22]

> I wish I were Commander in Chief in India ... I should do my utmost to exterminate the race upon whom the stain of the late cruelties rested ... and raze it off the face of the Earth.[23]

The ringleaders of the revolt were shot apart from cannons. Dickens's rather unhinged comments were contrasted with the attitude of the Governor-General of India, Charles Canning (1812–62). Canning advocated mercy by arguing that only those Sepoys who were directly involved in the rebellion should be punished, while the Sepoys who had merely deserted should be given an amnesty. This opinion earned him the derisory nickname of 'Clemency Canning' in the British and Anglo-Indian press. The government had to take further action however, and in 1858 the Company was wound up and the British government established direct rule over India with the passage of the Government of India Act. A proclamation 'To the Princes, Chiefs, and People of India' was issued after the India Act gained Royal Assent. Canning was no longer Governor-General but was now styled 'Viceroy'. The proclamation promised no further encroachments on the territory of the princely states; to respect the religion and customs of Indians; and to admit Indians into the civil service. Finally, in 1876, Queen Victoria was declared Empress of India.

The British did not stop at India but also made inroads into Africa, which Europeans called the 'Dark Continent' because its interior remained largely unexplored by them. The British had had encounters with Africans much earlier, but their activities were largely restricted to coastal areas, from where slaves were bought and then shipped over to plantations in America. Some explorers such as Mungo Park (1771–1806) did make excursions into central Africa, but for much of the eighteenth and early nineteenth centuries, diseases such as malaria, which struck down white colonists in great numbers, prevented any meaningful exploration of the interior. It was only after the anti-malarial drug quinine was marketed for use after 1854 that Europeans could venture into the continent with less fear of succumbing to disease. Park's expedition was sponsored by the African Association and tasked with seeking out potential new markets, as well as gathering knowledge for knowledge's sake about Africa's wildlife and people. By the mid-Victorian period, exploration of the continent was also bound up with Britain's new civilising mission: explorers and missionaries such as David Livingstone (1813–73) and Henry Morton Stanley (1841–1904) sought to, in Stanley's own words, was to 'flash a torch of light across ... this dark continent'.[24] While missionaries wanted to Christianise Africa, to entrepreneurs the continent, while largely undeveloped by European standards, was resource-rich and ripe for exploitation. And exploit it they did: every major European empire during the late-nineteenth century wanted a piece of the African cake. At the Berlin Conference in 1884, the continent was divided up between the United Kingdom, France, Belgium, Spain, Portugal, and of course Germany. There was not a single representative from any African community or nation present at this conference, which was a solely European affair (the United States attended and agreed to the terms of the conference, although they did not claim any territory themselves). After the conference, European powers established direct rule over a number of regions in Africa, and laid the foundations for many of its countries' borders today.

Between 1884 and 1918, the era of 'new' imperialism, the British Empire reached the height of its power. This period is so-called because it signalled a self-conscious effort on the part of European governments to embark on colonial projects and impose direct rule on far-flung places. What began as a largely entrepreneurial enterprise, with trading companies driving British commercial expansion, by the nineteenth century had become a state-sponsored endeavour supported by a powerful military and navy. Britannia truly 'ruled the waves' in the late-Victorian era.

Historians still debate the extent to which imperialism affected British culture back home. There are now two 'camps', so to speak, of empire historians. One group, which we might say hold to the 'older' view of this matter, maintain that imperialism had little effect upon British culture. The second group, who are proponents of 'new' imperial history, maintain that imperialism was to varying degrees diffused into every part of British society and culture. Even though support for the empire was never unanimous among the British public, quite clearly we must side with the second group of 'new' imperial historians in this matter.

At each step of the way, developments in the formation of the British Empire, from its beginnings in the late medieval period to the nineteenth century, generated a cultural response from intellectuals, journalists, novelists, poets, and artists. The deeds, or misdeeds, of imperialists were told to people in chapbooks, broadsides, newspapers, and most importantly in books. Let us examine, then, the rise of imperialist literature in the 1800s.

Chapter 2

Wholesome and Amusing Literature

"I loved those books that other boys love and I love them still. I well remember a little scene which took place when I was a child of eight or nine. *Robinson Crusoe* held me in its grasp and I was expected to go to church. I hid beneath a bed with *Robinson Crusoe* and was in due course discovered by an elder sister and governess, who, on my refusing to come out, resorted to force. Then followed a struggle that was quite Homeric. The two ladies tugged as best they might, but I clung to Crusoe and the legs of the bed, and kicked till, perfectly exhausted, they took their departure in no very Christian frame of mind, leaving me panting indeed, but triumphant."

H. Rider Haggard

Most people in the West today can afford to buy books. While prices for brand new hardback books can be somewhat expensive, if people are not willing to shell out approximately £30 for a copy of a work on its first release, they can be sure that it will soon come down in price significantly in a sale or even released as a cheap paperback after a few months. Yet for much of the nineteenth century, books were very expensive. The printing and binding processes were costly and much different to today. Each letter had to be carefully set – a process known as typesetting – which was incredibly time consuming and involved the labour of a number of apprentices. Publishers could order stereotypes of certain books to be made, which were casts of whole pages, but this was only a cost-effective option if they could be assured of a book's commercial potential. The printers then sold books in cardboard 'boards' and it would be up to the purchaser to take the books to a binders and have them bound according to his or her personal specification. Each book which survives from the eighteenth and early nineteenth centuries is therefore a unique object. To a modern collector, no two first editions of a book from that period will look the same in outward appearance.

THE SURGEON'S DAUGHTER.

The title page and frontispiece to Walter Scott's *The Surgeon's Daughter* (1827), in which the protagonists all find themselves in India due to changing circumstances. It was a very expensive novel to buy, much like many novels in this era, which would have set even lower middle-class buyers back about half a week's wages.

Adding to the cost of many novels was the fact that most of them were sold in two or three volumes. A novel such as Sir Walter Scott's *Surgeon's Daughter* which was part of his *Chronicles of the Canongate* retailed at 31s 6d. The high price was not simply because *The Surgeon's Daughter* was written by the 'Northern Wizard'; works by less famous authors retailed at similar prices. The price for Lady Sidney Owenson's *The Missionary: An Indian Tale* (1811) was £1 1s. Anne C. Monkland's *Life in India; or, The English at Calcutta* (1828) sold for 28s 6d. William B. Hockley's *The Zenana; or, a Nuwab's Leisure Hours* (1827) was 24s, as was his *Padurang Hari; or, Life of a Hindoo* (1826). So expensive were books that in 1818, one publisher told a House of Commons Select Committee that

> Books are a luxury, and the purchase of them has been confined to fewer people ... those who would be disposed to purchase books, have not the means of so doing, and are obliged to be frugal.[1]

In the early nineteenth century, skilled tradesmen and artisans would earn fifteen to twenty-five shillings per week, bricklayers and labourers ten to twelve,[2] and work was often casual or seasonal.[3] Purchasing the latest three-volume book for 31 shillings would not have been high on most working people's list of priorities.

Poorer readers were not totally bereft of literature however, for there was a flourishing trade in chapbooks and broadside ballads. The former were small pamphlets consisting of between 8 and 24 pages. They were usually sold for a penny or a half penny by street sellers who hawked their wares in towns and villages. Broadside ballads were single sheets

Sir Walter Scott, one of the most popular novelists of the early nineteenth century. Known as 'The Northern Wizard', he wrote a number of historical novels, most of them set in either eighteenth-century Scotland or in the Middle Ages.

of paper, roughly the same size as a tabloid newspaper today, with song lyrics on both sides. While many people indeed sang the lyrics from broadside ballads – either to a specified tune or awkwardly fitting the lyrics to another one they knew – people also read them as literature, and often read them aloud to each other. Henry Mayhew, in *London Labour and the London Poor* (1851), records that poor families would often club together to buy the latest broadside which they would then read aloud to each other.

Both broadsides and chapbooks often featured a crude woodcut which the publishers often recycled from earlier chapbooks – a woodcut depicting an old maid could also serve as the illustration for an Indian person in a song called *Revenge on India*, which calls for revenge on Indians after the revolt of 1857:

> I heard from the shore of India [sic] hot climate
> The shrill cry of murder steal on the air,
> Our friends call for aid and soon they shall find it
> For stout hearts and willing are hastening there,
> For England sweet isle of the rose and the lion,
> The birth place of valour their hope is in thee,
> Send thy warriors forth and their courage to rely on,
> And our sisters in peril they soon will set free.
>
> Oh Shall it be said they have tarnish'd the glory,
> And humbled the pride of Britannia's son's
> Brave hearts think of those whose body's [sic] lay gory,
> At Cawnpore and bleaching beneath the fierce son,
> Shall the fiends whose black crimes have wrung from each nation,
> With mercy be treated while there is men in the land,
> Who will boldly stand forth whatever their station,
> And fight for our honour with heart and with hand.

This is not great song writing. Set to the tune of D.J. Garrick's *The Soldier's Wife*, the lyrics were an awkward fit. The grammar and punctuation is likewise of a low standard. Still, even with the mismatched illustration and bad lyrics it would have found a ready audience among the poorer classes.

A broadside seller as depicted in Henry Mayhew's
London Labour and the London Poor (1851). Broadsides
ballads were single sheets of cheaply-printed paper
which contained the lyrics of a song and were sold for
either 1d or 1/2 d.

LONG-SONG SELLER.
"Two under fifty for a fardy'!"

While chapbooks and broadsides
reprinted songs, many also told short
stories; the latter were often published
by missionary societies to educate
poorer readers in Britain about the
people of far-flung lands. As we might
expect, these societies' depictions of
the indigenous people of overseas
territories was as a barbaric and
uncivilised people. *A Dialogue between
Farmer Trueman and his Son George
about the Cannibals in India* (c. 1800)
presents the inhabitants of various
islands in the Indian Ocean as savage
brutes:

> *George.* Father, what is a cannibal?
> *Father.* A cannibal, George, is a man eater.
> *G.* I have seen a picture of some wild Hottentots, eating the raw flesh of animals, but I never before heard of men eating one another.
> *F.* It is very true, although you may not have heard of it before.
> *G.* Indeed father, if you did not tell me so, I should not believe it; are there any such savages in this country?
> *F.* No, my dear, this horrid custom prevails in parts abroad, and particularly at Sumatra, and other Eastern Islands.[4]

The 'dialogue' format of this text recalls the moralist literature of the
early modern period. Clergymen would use this medium to warn against
the dangers of sin. The repentance of a sinner usually occurs as a result of

the debate between the upright man and the recalcitrant, ungodly man. Eventually the clergyman's words would convince the sinner of the need to repent of whatever sin he was guilty. Likewise, the dialogue between young George and his father, published by a religious tract society at a time when missionaries were beginning to be quite bothersome towards colonial officials, had a didactic message to fulfil: the pamphlet concludes that the only way in which these sinful 'savages' can be lifted out of their present state of barbarism is through the spreading of the gospel. There were some isolated reports of cannibalism in some colonies, just as there

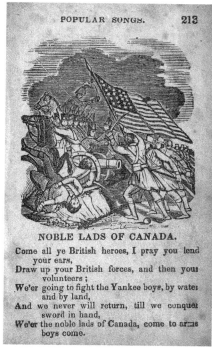

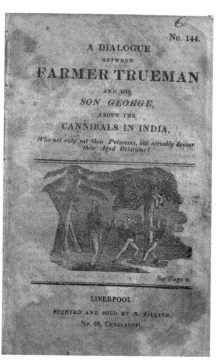

A popular song from the early 1800s entitled *Ye Noble Lads of Canada*, celebrating Canada's 'victory' during the War of 1812. These songs were printed on broadsides and could be had for as little as a penny. The lyrics can vary slightly but the message remains unchanged: the Canadians were proud of their British heritage.

Not every chapbook or broadside printed contained song lyrics. This one about a man named Farmer Trueman telling his son about alleged cases of cannibalism in India was printed by an evangelical society who aimed not only to educate the British working poor in Britain but also to justify their imperialist civilising mission.

have been cases within the British Isles, but missionaries very often over-sensationalised these accounts. Although the people of far-flung lands were quite shrewd; they often pretended to be cannibals to scare colonialists away, as the people of Fiji did in the eighteenth century.

Chapbook and ballad adaptations of *Robinson Crusoe* appeared in the early nineteenth century. Crusoe is a prototype of the British imperialist: he is a Christian and an entrepreneur who 'civilises' and cultivates the island on which he is marooned. He defends himself against hostile natives, named Caribs, who are also cannibals, and he acquires a servant in the form of Man Friday, whom he eventually converts to Christianity. Interestingly, the ballad version focuses more on the shipwreck and ensuing adventure rather than on any explicitly imperial concerns:

> When I was a lad, my fortune was bad,
> My grandfather I did lose, O!
> I'll bet you a can you have heard of the man,
> His name it was Robinson Crusoe.
> Oh! Poor Robinson Crusoe,
> Tinky ting tang, tinky ting tang,
> Oh! Poor Robinson Crusoe!
>
> You've read in a book of a voyage he took,
> While the raging whirlwinds blew so;
> That the ship with a shock fell plump on a rock,
> Near drowning poor Robinson Crusoe.
> Oh! Poor, &c.
>
> Poor soul! None but he escap'd on the sea,
> Ah! Fate! Fate! How could you so?
> Till at length he was thrown on an island unknown,
> Which received poor Robinson Crusoe.
> Oh! Poor, &c.
>
> But he sav'd from on board a gun and a sword,
> And another odd matter or two, so!
> That by dint of his thrift he manag'd to shift,

Pretty well for poor Robinson Crusoe.
Oh! Poor, &c.

While his man Friday kept the house snug and tidy,
To be sure 'twas his business to do so,
They liv'd friendly together, less like servant than neighbour,
Liv'd Friday and Robinson Crusoe.
Oh! Poor, &c.

Then he wore a large cap and a coat without nap,
And a beard as long as a Jew, so,
That by all that's civil, he looked like a devil,
More than poor Robinson Crusoe.
Oh! Poor, &c.

At length within hail, he saw a stout sail,
And he took to his little canoe so;
When he reach'd the ship, they gave him a trip
Back to England brought Robinson Crusoe.
 Oh! Poor, &c.[5]

Portrait of Daniel Defoe (1660–1731), the author of several novels whose protagonists ventured into the colonies. His first novel *Robinson Crusoe* (1719), which is widely regarded by scholars as being the very first English novel, sees the title marooned on a desert island having to fend for himself. He 'civilises' and cultivates the island, acquires a servant in the form of Man Friday, defends his island territory against cannibals, and returns to England as a rich man. He is the prototype of the British imperialist.

An important point should be recognised here: just because a certain story is set in the empire does not necessarily mean that it is promoting imperialism. Songs about the punishment of transportation rarely extolled the benefits of overseas settlement. A broadside entitled *The Sorrowful Lamentation of Benjamin Smith* (1816) tells the story of a man who was caught poaching and sentenced to death, but who subsequently had his punishment commuted to transportation.[6] The ballad of *The London 'Prentice Boy* likewise told a similar story, highlighting the lad's descent into sin and urging would-be criminals to avoid making the mistakes which had seen him end up in the penal colony of Van Dieman's Land:

> Come all you wild young chaps that live both far and near,
> Pray listen with attention to these few lines you'll hear,
> I once at ease did ramble but sin did me decoy,
> So now upon Van Dieman's Land is the London prentice boy.

The moral message was the all-important takeaway from these ditties. Transportation was hard, not just upon the convicted felon, but also upon their family. *The Sorrowful Lamentation of the Unhappy Men in Bristol* (c. 1832) asks readers to have sympathy with all who suffered from these felons' crimes:

> There is nineteen more transported,
> To a foreign land for life,
> Banished from their tender parents,
> From their children and wife:
> Lord ease the parents' troubled mind,
> Dry up the children's tears,
> Have pity on the weeping wife,
> And banish all her fears.

Benjamin Smith and *The London 'Prentice Boy* are sung to quite sombre tunes but other ballad writers had a more light-hearted approach to transportation. A song entitled *Ten Thousand Miles Away* (c. 1830) tells, to a surprisingly upbeat tune, the story of a man who longs to see his transported wife again:

Oh, that was a dark and dismal day, when I last saw my Peg,
She had a government band around each hand and another one
    round each leg;
Another one around each leg my boys; togged in a suit of grey,
Good-bye said she, remember me, ten thousand miles away.[7]

Other songs from the period tell of lovers separated when one of them
is called away to serve in the navy, one example being *Black-Eyed Susan*.
The poem was originally written by the playwright and popular ballad
enthusiast John Gay in 1720. Little did Gay know that this song would
be set to music and become one of the most popular ballads for the next
150 or so years (it is still performed by folk singers today). All ballads tell
a story, and *Black-Eyed Susan* recounts the tale of a sailor named William
who has briefly returned to his home town, and his wife Susan is there
to greet him. Sadly for the couple this is to be a flying visit for William:

> Though battles call me from thy arms,
> Let not my pretty Susan mourn;
> Though cannons roar, yet safe from harms,
> William shall to his dear return;
> Love turns aside the balls that round me fly,
> Lest precious tears should drop from Susan's eyes.

William then tells her of how at every beautiful sight he will likely see on
his journey he will think of his sweetheart:

> If to fair India's coast we sail,
> Thine eyes are seen in diamonds bright,
> Thy breath in Afric's spicy gale,
> Thy skin is ivory, so white,
> Thus ev'ry beauteous object that I view,
> Wakes in my soul, some charms of lovely Sue.[8]

The lyrics to *Black-Eyed Susan* are interesting because the sailor featured
does not attempt to mask the hardships of a seafaring life. Naval service in
Black-Eyed Susan was not about duty or patriotism, it is simply something

The song *Black-Eyed Susan*, originally written in the 1700s by John Gay, tells of Susan's brief but tearful meeting with her lover who in the Royal Navy. The pair enjoy only a few minutes together before he is called away again to serve. The story soon became a 'multimedia' event; as well as remaining a popular broadside ballad in the nineteenth century, it also featured in toy theatres and pantomimes.

BLACK EYED SUSAN.

All in the Downs the fleet lay moor'd,
The streamers waving in the wind,
When black ey'd Susan came on board:
Oh ! where shall I my true love find ?
Tell me, ye jovial sailors, tell me true,
If my sweet William sails among your crew.

William, who high upon the yard,
Rock'd by the billows to and fro,
Soon as her well-known voice he heard,
He sigh'd, and cast his eyes below ;
The cord slides swiftly thro' his glowing hands,
And quick as lightning, on the deck he stands.

So the sweet lark, high pois'd in air,
Shuts close his pinions to his breast,
If chance his mate's shrill voice to hear,
And drops, at once, into her nest.
The noblest captain in the British fleet,
Might envy William's lips those kisses sweet.

he is obligated to do. Indeed, when the song first appeared in the eighteenth century, the Impress Service, or 'the Press Gang', was in full force. Under the terms of this antiquated Elizabethan statute, this form of naval conscription allowed the authorities to 'press into service' any able-bodied man between the ages of 15 and 55, and

THE PENNY MAGAZINE

OF THE

Society for the Diffusion of Useful Knowledge.

55.]   PUBLISHED EVERY SATURDAY.   [FEBRUARY 9, 1833.

CHARMERS OF SERPENTS.

[Indian Jugglers exhibiting tamed Snakes.]

THERE are several passages in Scripture which allude to the commonly-received opinion in the East, that serpents are capable of being rendered docile, or at least harmless, by certain charms or incantations. The most remarkable of these texts is that of the 58th Psalm, where the wicked are compared to " the deaf adder that stoppeth her ear, which will not hearken to the voice of charmers, charming never so wisely;" and that of the 8th chapter of Jeremiah, " I will send serpents, cockatrices, among you, which will not be charmed." Dr. Shaw says that a belief that venomous serpents might be rendered innoxious by songs or muttered words, or by writing sentences or combinations of numbers upon scrolls of paper, prevailed through all those parts of Barbary where he travelled. In India, at the present day, the serpent-charmers are a well-known division of the numerous caste of jugglers that are found in every district. Mr. Forbes, in his ' Oriental Memoirs,' appears to attach some credit to their powers of alluring the *Cobra-di-Capello*, and other snakes, from their hiding-places, by the attraction of music. Mr. Johnson, however, in his ' Sketches of India Field Sports,' says, " The professed

resembling an Irish bagpipe, on which they play a plaintive tune. The truth is, this is all done to deceive. If ever a snake comes out of a hole at the sound of their music, you may be certain that it is a tame one, trained to it, deprived of its venomous teeth, and put there for the purpose; and this you may prove, as I have often done, by killing the snake, and examining it, by which you will exasperate the men exceedingly."

The account of Mr. Johnson certainly appears the more probable version of this extraordinary story; yet enough remains to surprise, in the wonderful command which these people possess over the reptiles that they have deprived of their power of injury, and taught to erect themselves and make a gentle undulating movement of the head, at certain modulated sounds. There can, we think, be no doubt that the snake is taught to do this, as the bear and the cock of the Italians are instructed to dance, as described in our last number. The jugglers are very expert in the exercise of the first branch of the trade, that of catching the snakes. They discover the hole of the reptile with great ease and certainty, and digging into it, seize the animal by the tail, with the left

Charles Knight's *Penny Magazine*, which ran from 1832 until 1845 with the aim of educating working and lower middle-class readers. The articles themselves are quite dry and 'encyclopaedic'. What was really special about this magazine, however, was the detailed illustrations on the front page. Through such images, people who might never have travelled abroad were able to view the sights of places from around the world.

often their targets were petty criminals or 'idle apprentices', most of whom were from poorer stations in society. It is likely that William in the song is among those who had been impressed into service due to the song's later reference to 'landsmen'. 'Landsman' was a naval slang word applied by professional sailors to unqualified pressed men like William who, until having been caught by the gangs, had never been to sea before. William will also face other hardships and privations: cannons will roar beside him, and although he will endeavour to make it back home, there is no guarantee that he will. The song ends with the lovers bidding each other 'adieu'; contemporary listeners would not have known whether the pair were ever reunited. In an era when sea voyages could take months, and the colonies due to the climate and disease were dangerous places, such scenes must have been all-too-familiar sights at ports.

The question on most pamphleteers' minds in the early nineteenth century was domestic politics. The middle and working classes demanded political reform through universal suffrage and an end to the Corn Laws which were tariffs on imports of grain; these laws kept the price of bread artificially high and protected the interests of the landowners' inefficient farming businesses. In tandem with the campaign for political reform led by celebrity speakers such as Henry Hunt (1773–1835), there was a steady stream of chapbooks and pamphlets published at this time which were openly critical of the political establishment. Perhaps the biggest-selling cheap pamphlet in the early part of the century was William Hone's *The Political House that Jack Built* (1819). This was an attack on the political establishment in the aftermath of the Peterloo Massacre at Manchester, when the magistrates called the local yeomanry out on a crowd of 60,000 peaceful pro-democracy demonstrators.

But beginning in the 1830s, a number of cheap literary magazines appeared on the scene which were often sponsored by some society dedicated to improving the manners and morals of the working classes through education: *The Saturday Magazine*, *The Edinburgh Journal*, and Charles Knight's *Penny Magazine*. Chief among these was the latter, funded by the rather pompously named Society for the Diffusion of Useful Knowledge, and featured essays on British history and pieces on general knowledge. To a modern reader, its articles, while informative, are a bit of a dry read and sound as though they were written for an encyclopaedia. What was really special about the magazine were the numerous illustrations. Through the images, which were of high quality in contrast to those which appeared in the cheap chapbooks, working-class readers saw images of the empire and its people and wildlife, such as the Inuit people of British North America, snake charmers from the Indian subcontinent, and lions from Africa. For poorer readers, it was the chapbooks, broadsides, and penny magazines that provided them with a glimpse of the empire.

Novelists in the early-Victorian period were more concerned with the 'Condition of England' question than they were with the British Empire. The 1830s and '40s witnessed the emergence of the Victorian social novel which drew attention to the hardships faced by many people in the modern industrial city. Charles Dickens's *Oliver Twist* (1838) is a prime example, dealing as it does with the effects of the recently passed Poor Law Amendment Act (1834), which expanded the workhouse system. The empire is referenced in Dickens's novel inasmuch as the Artful Dodger is sentenced to transportation, but there are few imperial overtones in the story. The same is true for other novels published during the mid-Victorian period: references are incidental and the colonies are usually places to where the bad characters are shipped off, usually forcibly. Sometimes a character is shipped off to the colonies to keep them away from a lover whose parents disapprove of the match, much like what happens to Mr Percy in G.W.M. Reynolds's *Master Timothy's Bookcase* (1842).

Some mid-Victorian novels depict colonists as living a 'Crusoesque' life. An example of this was R.M. Ballantyne's *The Young Fur Traders* (1856). The young protagonist, Charlie, lives in British North America and desires to live 'like Robinson Crusoe ... to fight with redskins and grizzly bears, and chase the buffaloes over miles and miles of prairies on rough nags'.[9] Ballantyne wrote many novels which were set overseas, but in most of his works there was little in the way of jingoistic patriotism which was characteristic of novels in the late 1800s.

The empire was almost like a dirty little secret for some novelists, much like Mr Rochester in Charlotte Brontë's *Jane Eyre* (1847), who keeps his mad wife Bertha locked in the attic; Bertha was a Jamaican woman who had a discoloured and 'savage-looking' face. The empire was a fact of life which, for them to inject some social realism into their plots, authors would have had to acknowledge in some manner but they were not necessarily promoting the British Empire.

Works by American novelists were just as easily available in Britain. Due to the fact that there were few, if any, international copyright agreements at this time British publishers did not have to pay foreign writers any royalties. Pirated copies of popular works by American authors were a lucrative source of income for many printers. Such was the case with James Fenimore Cooper's *The Last of the Mohicans: A Narrative of 1757* (1826), a novel set in what is now upstate New York during the Seven Years' War. Reviewers in Britain were certainly impressed with the novel: *The Monthly Review* declared that Fenimore Cooper was almost as talented as Walter Scott. However, they still printed their books in the expensive three volume format, and a first British edition of *The Last of the Mohicans* would have set a purchaser back £1 1s.

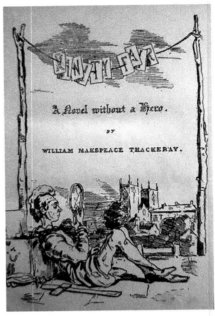

Title page to William Makepeace Thackeray's *Vanity Fair: A Novel without a Hero* (1848) in which readers meet Joseph Sedley, a 'Nabob' who works for the East India Company, and Captain Dobbin, who disappears off to India once he realises that he will forever be unlucky in love.

Books remained expensive into the mid-Victorian period. Hardback editions of Dickens's novels were published in the same three volume format and sold at similar prices to Scott's novels. The expensive price of books caused one contemporary reviewer in 1843 to remark that, even among the middle classes, 'there are very few who purchase novels when they are first published'.[10] Many people borrowed the latest popular novel from one of the many subscription libraries. To satisfy middle–class readers' demand for new novels, the subscription libraries purchased large quantities of them. Mudie's Circulating Library, to take one example, ordered 2,000 copies of George Elliot's *The Mill on the Floss*

(1860), while between 1853 and 1862, Mudie added 416,706 copies of various new novels to his library.

Another way that readers could avoid paying for expensive books outright was by purchasing the latest instalment in a magazine. Although the serialisation of novels is rarely pursued as a business model by publishing houses today, Victorian printing houses adopted this practice because it enabled them to assess the commercial viability of a novel before investing funds into the production of hardbound editions. *Oliver Twist* was serialised in weekly parts in *Bentley's Miscellany* in 1838 and Thackeray's *Vanity Fair* (1847–48) was sold in one shilling parts. In Thackeray's novel, as is the case in the works of Dickens, the empire features but has only a marginal place. Readers meet two characters who are connected to British India: the obese and vain Joseph Sedley, an East India Company nabob, and there is Captain Dobbin, who disappears off to India when he realises that his love for a woman named Amelia will remain unrequited.

Where Victorian readers could not afford a shilling copy of the latest instalment of Thackeray's *Vanity Fair*, they might have opted to purchase one of the many serialised penny novels which were in circulation. These appeared both as stand-alone novels and were also printed in magazines such as *The London Journal*, *The People's Periodical and Family Library*, and *Reynolds's Miscellany*, to name but a few. The popularity of such literature is indicated in the following remarks by Charles Knight who, although he detested the public's voracious appetite for popular literature, found that its popularity spanned a variety of classes and trades:

> In every shop in every back-street of London and the larger towns, where a tradesman in tobacco or lollipops or Lucifer matches formerly grew thin upon his small amount of daily half-pence, there now rush in the schoolboy, the apprentice, the milliner, the factory girl, the clerk, and the small shopkeeper, for their 'London Journal', 'Family Herald', and 'Cassell's Paper'.[11]

Two of the most popular penny novelists in this genre were G.W.M. Reynolds (1814–79) and his friend Pierce Egan the Younger (1814–80). In contrast to Dickens's bourgeois novels-with-a-social-conscience, novels

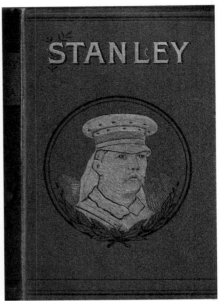

These are just a few examples of the many decorative children's and young adult books which were immensely popular in the latter part of the nineteenth century. George Alfred Henry, whose *True to the Old Flag* is featured here, was the author of over thirty books, most of which were set in the colonies.

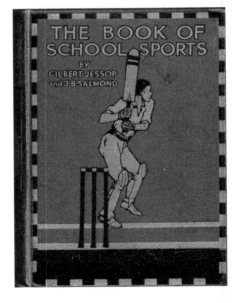

written by Egan and Reynolds were political but usually had a healthy dose of sex and violence, with one commentator in *The Times* criticising them for being full of 'lust' and 'murder'.[12] Reynolds was highly critical of imperialism in the newspaper which he owned and edited, *Reynolds's*

THE BOY'S OWN PAPER

No. 821.—Vol. XVII.   SATURDAY, OCTOBER 6, 1894.   Price One Penny.
[ALL RIGHTS RESERVED.]

AMID SIBERIAN FORESTS.

A TALE OF THE RUSSIAN
CONQUEST OF ASIA.

BY DAVID KER,

*Author of "Captives of the Ocean," "Unseen Depths,"
"Afloat in a Volcano," etc.*

(*With Illustrations by H. M. Paget.*)

"He saw by a glance at his fallen enemy that the work was done."

The Boy's Own Journal: one of the most popular boys' magazines from the late-Victorian era. Instalments of new novels were featured in its columns every week. As well as this, boys also had their own 'problem page' where they could write in with queries on a variety of subjects. Several public school masters wrote articles giving fitness advice. Young lads could, if they wish, submit their own poetry (though it was often of very bad quality). It was intended as an antidote to the more controversial penny dreadful magazines which flourished during the same period.

Newspaper. The empire likewise featured in Reynolds's ground-breaking novel *The Mysteries of London*. In one part of the book, the notorious villain, Crankey Jem, is sent to an Australian penal colony. Even in Reynolds's novel, however, the empire was simply a fact of life, as it was in the works of Dickens and Brontë, and as we shall see in chapter eight, Reynolds certainly did not promote imperialism.

These salacious penny novels or 'bloods', after they completed their serial runs, were bound as complete works in 'Library Editions' which suited the pockets of more affluent purchasers. Reynolds's *Mysteries of London*, for instance, was published in four volumes, and each volume retailed individually for 6s 6d. Still, something had to be done so that authors such as Dickens could sell their novels in volume form for a relatively cheap price to the lower middle and working classes. The turning point came in the late 1840s and 1850s. The invention of the railway, and the extension of the rail network throughout England, had an unintended effect on the price of books. In earlier times, travellers journeyed by horse-drawn coaches. These rides were so bumpy and uncomfortable, and the interiors of the coaches often so dark, that only the most dedicated readers would attempt to read a novel while making their journey. The railways, in contrast, were brightly lit and a much more pleasant and smoother ride. It was the perfect opportunity for people to catch up on the latest novel. So in 1849, Routledge began issuing one shilling paperback novels as part of their 'Railway Library' range, which colloquially became known as 'yellowbacks'. The poorest of the poor probably did not purchase these editions but they were cheaper than the 31 shilling novel. Other publishers recognised that Routledge was onto a winning formula and began issuing similar publications, and by 1893 one commentator remarked that,

> The clerks and artisans, shopgirls, dressmakers, and milliners, who pour into London every morning by the early trains, have, each and every one, a choice specimen of penny fiction with which to beguile the short journey, and perhaps the few spare minutes of a busy day. The workingman who slouches up and down the platform, waiting for the moment of departure, is absorbed in some crumpled bit of pink-covered romance. The girl who lounges opposite to us in the

carriage, and who would be a very pretty girl in any other conceivable hat, sucks mysterious sticky lozenges, and reads a story.[13]

In the same year that Routledge launched its Railway Library, a Select Committee began inquiring into the feasibility of launching public lending libraries as part of a drive to guide the working classes towards more respectable forms of 'rational recreation'. Lending libraries had existed before this, but they were subscription-based and their works were usually accessible only to the bourgeoisie and aristocracy. Although the working classes worked long hours even in 1849, workers had much more leisure time compared to earlier generations and some moral campaigners were worried about how they might be spending their time – they certainly did not want the masses wiling away their few hours of freedom in the public house! After much wrangling in parliamentary circles, the Public Libraries Act was passed in 1850. The Act left a lot to be desired: it only required towns with a population of over 10,000 people to erect a library and there was little financial provision made for the purchasing of books. Most MPs and government ministers believed that charitable donations and cast-offs from subscription libraries would be enough to fill the shelves. Nevertheless, the Act was a step in the right direction, and over the next century public libraries began to appear over the length and breadth of the country.

By the 1850s then, novels were becoming more affordable and, even where they could not be purchased outright, at least more accessible because of the establishment of public libraries. Novels from the earlier part of the century did feature the empire to some extent, but Charles Kingsley's *Westward Ho* (1855) marked the real turning point in national culture, as literary works began to turn their attention to colonial themes and promoted imperialist ideology. This was concomitant with the gradual shift in government policy from informal imperial rule, conducted through trading companies, to the creation of a more formalised empire, which would continue apace after the Indian Mutiny in 1857 and the Berlin Conference in 1884. Many of the tropes which appear in late-Victorian imperial fiction appeared in Kingsley's novel, which follows the adventures of a young boy who joins Sir Francis Drake on an expedition to South America. As we will see, G.A. Henty (1832–1902), the later Victorian author and all-round imperial cheerleader, followed this model in most of his novels, which often depicted a young lad becoming involved in the adventures of a famous imperialist from British history.

The emerging genre of imperial hardback fiction had to compete against another more controversial form of fiction: the penny dreadful. Earlier in the nineteenth century, penny bloods had provided cheap, violent and sexualised entertainment to adult readers. After the 1860s, some publishers decided to provide similar entertainment specifically for children and young adult readers. These dreadfuls were weekly or monthly serials and usually told the stories of famous criminals and pirates from England and overseas. The Australian highwayman Ned Kelly (1854–80) was a well-liked figure in these serials, as well as the roguish young lad Jack Harkaway

H. Rider Haggard avidly read Defoe's *Robinson Crusoe* in his youth and went on to write a number of phenomenally popular adventure novels that were set in the colonies including *King Solomon's Mines* (1885) and *She* (1887). Of all of the late-Victorian adventure novelists, it is probably his works which have had the most longevity; both of the novels listed above have been adapted into movies and television series. His courageous explorer, Allen Quatermain, even provided the inspiration for Indiana Jones. This image was from a special feature on him featured in *The Graphic*, 9 July 1898.

whose adventures took him around the world. The popularity of penny dreadfuls threatened to eclipse the morally respectable works written by the likes of Henty and Ballantyne. Contemporary observers such as Charlotte Yonge (1823–1901) worried about the effects such magazines might have on the minds of impressionable youths:

Wholesome and amusing literature has become almost a necessity among the appliances of parish work. The power of reading leads, in most cases, to the craving for books. If good not be provided, evil will only too easily be found ... If the boy is not to betake himself to 'Jack

Sheppard' literature, he must be beguiled by wholesome adventure. If the girl is not to study the 'penny dreadful,' her notions must be refined by the tale of high romance or pure pathos.[14]

(Jack Sheppard was the name of a notorious boy thief who was hanged in 1724 but who enjoyed a 'literary afterlife' as the star of many Victorian novels and penny bloods). Penny dreadfuls were the 'video nasties' of their day, and even an organisation called the Pure Literature Society was set up to save youths from these evil magazines. Yonge was hardly a lone voice as other reviewers echoed her concerns regarding such dangerous literature:

> There is now before us such a verifiable mountain of pernicious trash, mostly in paper covers, and all 'Price One Penny': so-called novelettes, romances, tales, stories of adventure, mystery and crime; pictures of school life hideously unlike the reality; exploits of pirates, robbers, cut-throats, prostitutes, and rogues, that, but for its actual presence, it would seem incredible.[15]

One response to the penny dreadful was the publication of *The Boys' Own Magazine* in 1879. This magazine was illustrated, just like a penny dreadful, but its fiction was altogether more respectable than those 'lower' forms of literature. Within the columns of this weekly magazine were bland stories about schoolboy's days at Eton or some other celebrated public school, and the hero displayed the qualities of athleticism, patriotism, love of one's school, country, empire, and a good sense of fair play. There were also adventure stories which mimicked those found in the hardback books of Ballantyne, Kingsley, and Henty. Other respectable and patriotic penny periodicals soon followed such as *Chums* (1892–1941) and *Union Jack* (1894–1933).

Amusingly, some penny dreadfuls magazines had titles that sounded very similar to the respectable one such as *Boys of England, Sons of Britannia, Young Briton*. A fact that was often drawn attention to in newspaper reports on juvenile crime was that copies of these were found in the pockets of young offenders when they were arrested. When 13-year-old Alfred Saunders was arrested in January 1876 for stealing

£7 4s from his father, *The Times* reported that the arresting officer found that 'his pockets were crammed with copies of works such as *The Pirates League*, or *The Seagull*, the *Young Briton*, *Sons of Britannia*, and the *Boys of England*'. Such 'low' works were, in the eyes of many, responsible for leading them astray and the periodicals were scapegoated not only by the police force, but also the courts, and the press for the rise in juvenile crime.

Much of the criticism of penny dreadfuls was without foundation and merely the result of moral panic. To break their hold over youth's minds, respectable books would have to be exciting, look attractive, and relatively cheap. It is not until the late-Victorian era that we find mass market, clothbound, and highly decorative books appearing in shops and available via mail order. The technology to create decorative books with pictures on the front covers was actually developed in the 1830s when the process of binding books was mechanised, and binders found a specific type of cloth they could lay over cardboard boards that was easy to mechanically decorate through blind stamping. The stamps were then usually inlaid with gold and a variety of other colours. These developments in book decoration occurred in tandem with the invention of the rotary steam press in the United States in 1843. The rotary press made the production of the printed page itself a more streamlined and efficient process, enabling thousands of copies of a single page to be printed daily because the type on this press was placed on a large cylinder while paper was run underneath it. Publishing houses in the United Kingdom were initially slow to adopt this technology, so it was not until the 1860s that printing firms began to create truly mass market editions of literary works which looked nice. The attractive bindings of the books soon became a selling point. The following advert is typical of many which appeared in the back matter of books during the latter part of the century:

Perseverance Island: or, The Robinson Crusoe of the 19th Century.
By Douglas Frazar.
With 6 page illustrations.
New Edition. Crown 8vo, cloth elegant, 3s.[16]

(For readers unfamiliar with nineteenth-century print culture, '8vo' is an abbreviation for *octavo*. It refers to the size of the book and signifies that the publishers had folded a large folio-size sheet of paper eight times).[17] Many of these books ranged in price from three shillings to eight shillings, which suited the pockets of parents from a wide range of backgrounds, and thanks to improved overseas transportation on steam-powered ships, could with relative ease be shipped abroad. This made mass market books even more commercially viable as it broadened the publishers' potential market. Even where parents in Britain could not afford the books themselves, poorer children most likely received them as prizes for high achievement in schools or as gifts from their Sunday school teachers. Every literary historian who studies late-Victorian children's books will at some point in their careers have encountered an *ex libris* label pasted onto the front end papers indicating that they were given out as gifts.

Photograph of popular imperialist fiction author, George Alfred Henty, who wrote numerous adventure stories set in the colonies. To read one of his novels is to read them all: a school boy is usually encouraged to enlist in the army, and they find themselves at the centre of the action in some pivotal event in the rise of the British Empire.

While many of the books portraying heroes of the British Empire were undeniably targeted towards a younger readership, we should not assume that it was *only* children who read books written by Henty and others like him. A survey of over 800 adult manual labourers in Sheffield, conducted in 1918, revealed that the most popular authors and books among these men were

Ballantyne, Henty, *Robinson Crusoe*, *Quentin Dirward* [sic], *Ivanhoe*, *Waverley*, *Kidnapped*, *Treasure Island* and *Two Years before the Mast*, as well as the travels of David Livingstone, Fridtjof Nansen, Matthew Peary and Scott of the Antarctic.[18]

These labourers clearly had a liking for stories of adventure and tales of derring-do – much like adults attend cinema screenings of superhero and James Bond movies today – although we do have to wonder whether these people more often read these books with their children. After all, reading was both a private activity as well as a family pastime. Parents often read books to their children, much as they do nowadays.[19]

Teresa Michals has recently shown that there was a grey area between children's and adult literature and that young and old often read the same material. The works of H. Rider Haggard, for instance, were enjoyed by 'boys of all ages'. During the late-Victorian and Edwardian era, works which had previously been written for adults became staples of children's literature. A case in point is *Robinson Crusoe*, originally published in 1719 for adults but reprinted frequently throughout the nineteenth century in editions marketed specifically for children, even though adults continued to read it. By 1878, Leslie Stephen, writing in The *Cornhill Magazine*, confidently declared that *Robinson Crusoe* was 'a book for boys rather than men'.[20] For imperialists, Defoe's novel was highly influential: George Borrow deemed *Robinson Crusoe* so important that he gave Defoe credit for the expansion of the British Empire:

[*Robinson Crusoe*] was a book which has exerted over the minds of Englishmen an influence certainly greater than any other of modern times... a book from which the most luxuriant and fertile of our modern prose writers have drunk inspiration; a book, moreover, to which from the hardy deeds which it narrates, and the spirit of strange and romantic enterprise which it tends to awaken, England owes many of her astonishing discoveries both by sea and by land, and no inconsiderable part of her naval glory.[21]

The book's influence was undeniable: Young H. Rider Haggard, who went on to write a number of stories set in the colonies, recalled with fondness his youthful readings of *Robinson Crusoe* which verged upon the obsessive, much to the chagrin of his governess.[22] Clearly for young Rider Haggard, delving into an imaginary exotic island was much more exciting than sitting in a church!

Whenever one studies an ideology, which is essentially what this book is – the study of one aspect of *imperialism* – one must take account of the medium through which that ideology was disseminated. In the case of novels, we have to consider the book as a product first. Now we have considered how such works were published, let us venture into this 'empire of the imagination', to borrow a phrase from the all-powerful *She-Who-Must-Be-Obeyed*.[23]

Chapter 3

Play Up! Play Up! And Play the Game!

There's a breathless hush in the Close to-night –
Ten to make and the match to win –
A bumping pitch and a blinding light,
An hour to play and the last man in.
And it's not for the sake of a ribboned coat,
Or the selfish hope of a season's fame,
But his Captain's hand on his shoulder smote
"Play up! play up! and play the game!"

The sand of the desert is sodden red, –
Red with the wreck of a square that broke; –
The Gatling's jammed and the colonel dead,
And the regiment blind with dust and smoke.
The river of death has brimmed his banks,
And England's far, and Honour a name,
But the voice of schoolboy rallies the ranks,
"Play up! play up! and play the game!"

This is the word that year by year
While in her place the School is set
Every one of her sons must hear,
And none that hears it dare forget.
This they all with a joyful mind
Bear through life like a torch in flame,
And falling fling to the host behind –
"Play up! play up! and play the game!"

Henry Newbolt, *Vitae Lampada* (1897)

For as long as human societies have existed, people have always enjoyed playing sports. The inhabitants of Ancient China played a game that was similar to soccer which people play today. Ancient Greece had their Olympic Games and the Romans had their gladiatorial combats. The Byzantine Empire had its chariot races and on occasion its supporters even acted like modern-day football hooligans, if the Byzantine scholar Procopius is to be believed.[1] The upper classes in early modern England enjoyed hunting or cricket, while a rather rough version of football, or 'mob football', was played by the plebeian classes in towns and villages. There were also sports which all classes enjoyed watching together: in late eighteenth- and early nineteenth-century Britain, bare-knuckle boxing, or pugilism, was attended by high and low. Most people played or watched sports for enjoyment; athletes were rarely paid and there was little sense of a moral purpose behind the playing of sports. Sport and fitness were not a part of the school curriculum before the

Engraving of Rugby School in 1841, published in London by J. E. Harwood. Dr Thomas Arnold was appointed as Headmaster here and made several reforms to the curriculum, with the aim of turning unruly boys into Christian gentlemen. Image supplied with thanks to the Wellcome Library.

early part of the nineteenth century. The importance placed upon sport changed in the mid-Victorian period however, with the reform of the public schools, when the ideology of athleticism – strength, speed, power, resilience, and stamina – was promoted among public schoolboys by their teachers and to the public-at-large in popular literature.

Many public schools today lay claim to an ancient and historical heritage. King's School in Canterbury claims, with some justification, that it was established in the year 597. Many more schools were set up during the late medieval and early modern era as a response to the Reformation under Henry VIII. Where youths might have once been instructed by the Catholic Church in an abbey, after Henry's break with Rome and the dissolution of the monasteries, youths would now be instructed by tutors in schools affiliated with the newly-established Church of England.

Yet by the eighteenth century, the public schools' reputation was at rock bottom. The curriculum was dominated by the classics and while this may have been a good idea during the Reformation, when a familiarity with the works of Ancient Greek and Roman writers was highly valued, it was inadequate for the commercial world of Georgian England. Even if the lads learned anything meaningful in the classroom, their behaviour left much to be desired and bullying was rife. The colleges also had a reputation as hotbeds of vice and moral depravity, and as a result the upper middle classes of Georgian Britain largely avoided sending their sons to these places and preferred to educate their children at home. Parents were not wide of the mark: William Hickey (1749–1830) recalled that by the age of 14, when the school day had finished he and his fellows often visited taverns and brothels. The boys at some of these schools rose in revolt on more than one occasion. At Rugby in 1797 a riot broke out when the headmaster decided that sixth form students should pay for the damage they had inflicted on a local tradesman's property. At Eton in 1818, the boys rebelled against the headmaster, John Keate, and smashed up the desks and windows. On more than one occasion the militia had to be called to some of these schools to control the boys. In such a context, it is unsurprising that the tutors at these schools were often harsh taskmasters and did not flinch from meting out brutal corporal punishment to unruly boys.

Things improved when Dr Thomas Arnold became headmaster of Rugby in 1828. He did not amend the classics-based curriculum in any significant way but concerned himself with improving the boys' behaviour, and the reputation of the school, by giving the lads a good moral education. He allowed the students a limited degree of self-governance through the prefect system, which would teach the lads to take responsibility for their actions. Arnold also permitted the boys to play team sports, although these were not initially a formal part of the syllabus. Other public schools soon followed Arnold's lead in ensuring the boys' morals were improved and gradually placed a greater emphasis on sport and exercise. A pioneer in this regard was G.E.L. Cotton (1813–66), one of Arnold's former pupils who became headmaster of Marlborough School. Under Cotton, team games became a formalised part of the school curriculum which would allow boys to exhaust themselves on the pitch instead of rioting, going about town visiting taverns and brothels, like Hickey and his pals did in the preceding century. Harrow followed Cotton's lead, although it would take a Royal Commission in the 1860s to fully reform all of the schools by suggesting some practical changes updating the schools' curricula and moving away from the classics and also the formalisation of team games across the board. The reforms worked, and by the 1870s the public reputation of the schools had recovered and they became places which were respectable enough for the sons of the upper middle classes to be educated.

For most young middle-class boys, their education did not stop at leaving school for many of them went on to attend university. A 'special relationship' between the public schools, Oxbridge (where many boys went after finishing their schooling), and imperial service soon developed. The qualities cultivated in young boys at these institutions were good for the empire because they produced brave and tough soldiers, many of whom would be natural leaders due to their participation in team games and athletics.

Lest we give too much credit to the mid-Victorian public school masters for connecting sport and militarism however, we should note that writers in the earlier part of the century aired similar sentiments. In Pierce Egan the Elder's *Life in London and Sporting Guide* in 1824, he implied that, should any foreign power ever attempt an invasion of Britain, they could expect to be met by tough British boxers:

The public schools were fiercely proud of their ancient heritage. This is a commemorative print of Charterhouse alumni. Look closely and you can see the names of two men who feature prominently in this book: the novelist W. M. Thackeray, and the founder of the Scouts, Robert Baden–Powell. Image supplied with thanks to the Wellcome Library.

While such heroes as those are Britannia's boast,
We might still bid defiance to each foreign host;
And should our proud foes dare assault Britain's shore,
They might get as good millings as they've had before.
Then Britons rejoice and make the air ring,
In praise of our heroes, brave Langan and Spring.[2]

Messrs Langan and Spring were two Irish bare-knuckle boxers who became celebrities briefly in 1824 because of their victories in the ring. Writing in *Boxiana*, Egan the Elder argued that bare-knuckle boxing might help working men toughen up for the army lest they become effeminate and unable to fight in the army:

> It is of the very last importance to ENGLAND as a nation, my Lord, that not one particle of this real greatness should ever be frittered away from *squeamishness* of DISPOSITION or EFFEMINACY ... in order to prevent a WELLINGTON ... from ever experiencing the want of a body of brave men to direct.[3]

Walter Scott likewise recognised the seeming connection between fitness and success on the battlefield in *Waverley; or 'Tis Sixty Years Since* (1814), in which the protagonist Edward Waverley is treated to the spectacle of highlanders practising their exercises to ensure that they are fit enough to protect their country:

> There was a sight, however, before the gate, which perhaps would have afforded the first owner of Blenheim more pleasure than the finest view in the domain assigned to him by the gratitude of his country. This consisted of about a hundred Highlanders, in complete dress and arms; at sight of whom the Chieftain apologised to Waverley in a sort of negligent manner.
>
> "He had forgot," he said, "that he had ordered a few of his clan out, for the purpose of seeing that they were in a fit condition to protect the country, and prevent such accidents as, he was sorry to learn, had befallen the Baron of Bradwardine. Before they were dismissed, perhaps Captain Waverley might choose to see them go through a part of their exercise."

Edward assented, and the men executed with agility and precision some of the ordinary military movements. They then practised individually at a mark, and showed extraordinary dexterity in the management of the pistol and firelock. They took aim, standing, sitting, leaning, or lying prostrate, as they were commanded, and always with effect upon the target. Next, they paired off for the broadsword exercise; and, having manifested their individual skill and dexterity, united in two bodies, and exhibited a sort of mock encounter, in which the charge, the rally, the flight, the pursuit, and all the current of a heady fight, were exhibited to the sound of the great war bagpipe. On a signal made by the Chief, the skirmish was ended. Matches were then made for running, wrestling, leaping, pitching the bar, and other sports, in which this feudal militia displayed incredible swiftness, strength, and agility; and accomplished the purpose which their Chieftain had at heart, by impressing on Waverley no light sense of their merit as soldiers, and of the power of him who commanded them by his nod.

Adam Hartley, the hero of Scott's *The Surgeon's Daughter*, was 'of the genuine Saxon mould' and proficient in 'the rough exercises of wrestling, boxing, leaping, and quarter-staff, and when he could obtain leisure, the bull-baitings and football matches'.[4] Yet it was not enough to simply be brave on the turf or the battlefield, admirable though that was. One had to be able to remain cool under pressure and form a strategy for fighting to fight bravely and fight well, which is why Egan often appropriated the language of the battlefield and applied it to that of the ring and turf:

It might be asked, what is an admiral without tactics? Or, a General without scientific precision? And where it has appeared, that downright *force* has succeeded once – *skill*, it will be found, has produced victory a hundred times; courage would degenerate into mere ferocity, if not tempered with judgement.[5]

Perhaps as a result of the rise of the ideology of domesticity – of which we shall learn more in the third chapter – the association between physical prowess and military service in literature disappeared somewhat during the 1840s and 1850s. It was only with the promotion of sport

The public schools were not the first to associate physical fitness with military prowess. Pierce Egan in both his *Book of Sports* and *Boxiana* also argued that, for the country to maintain its international supremacy, British men would need to 'toughen up' so they could resist foreign invaders.

Robert Clive whose military exploits were instrumental in expanding British power in the Indian subcontinent. He enjoyed a posthumous 'literary afterlife' in a number of late-Victorian literary works and was regarded as one of the heroes of the empire, although radicals and socialists viewed his 'achievements' in a rather more negative light.

and fitness in the public schools in the mid-to-late nineteenth century that we find fitness, combined with imperialism, promoted once again in literary works. Those who did not attend the public schools were still urged to strive for the same levels of physical perfection as the boys from the public schools. A writer covering Rugby School's athletic sports in the *Boys' Own Annual* in 1865 urged 'many, many hundreds of English lads in other less distinguished sports [to] take pattern and example by the discipline and skill evinced by their brethren'.[6] Gilbert Jessop, writing in *The Book of School Sports* (c. 1920), told youths that the Great War was won on the playing grounds of Eton and also at 'every ground where a game is played'.[7] If youths of any social rank ensured they were physically fit, so these writers reasoned, they would be able to 'Play Up! Play Up! And Play the Game!' As Henty counselled readers in 1906, all lads should 'exercise [their] body in every way, so that [they] may grow up so strong and active [...and] so harden their frames that, in battle, the bravest peoples cannot stand against them.'[8]

Henty was a prolific novelist who between 1864 and his death wrote 122 books. All were historical novels and in one way or another heavily imbued with imperial ideology. A flavour of their imperialist tone can be seen when one examines their titles: *Under Drake's Flag* (1883); *By Sheer Pluck* (1884); *With Clive in India* (1884); *The Young Colonists* (1885).[9] Henty's novels, like those written by Kingsley and Ballantyne before him, often featured a schoolboy hero who finds himself caught up in some event that was pivotal in the rise of the British Empire, thrust into the midst of battle alongside famous men from imperial history. *With Clive in India* tells the story of young Charlie Marryat (the name of Marryat evokes the memory of the famous Frederick Marryat who served in the navy during the Napoleonic Wars and invented a signal code for merchant vessels). After Charlie's father dies, he is sent as an apprentice writer to the East India Company (a writer in the historical East India Company was stationed in the subcontinent and served the equivalent function of an accountant). Charlie has his sights set on bigger things than the life of a mere writer and soon secures a commission as an officer in the Company's army, where he serves under Robert Clive. The reader first meets Charlie before he sets out for India, and at the beginning Henty gives us a glimpse of young Charlie's athletic ability:

PROFESSOR BECKWITH AND HIS FAMILY

Professor Beckwith and his family pose in their swimming costumes for *The Boy's Own Annual* in 1865. This particular exercise was deemed to be most helpful in promoting boys' fitness; levels and, if an English lad could become a good swimmer, it would signal to the world, so it was thought, that he had become 'lord of creation' by mastering the elements.

He was slight in build, but his schoolfellows knew that Charlie Marryat's muscles were as firm and hard as those of any boy in the school. In all sports requiring activity and endurance, rather than weight and strength, he was always conspicuous. Not one in the school could compete with him in long distance running, and when he was one of the hares there was but little chance for the hounds. He was a capital swimmer, and one of the best boxers in the school.[10]

Contemporary writers showed how many British heroes of old, such as Beowulf, proved their physical prowess by being able to swim.[11] The sport was one means through which a lad might prove he was worthy of imperial service and membership of the British 'race'.[12] *The Boys' Own Annual* revealed that:

Swimming [is] an exercise which has every possible recommendation in its favour and not a single drawback. It is easy, it is healthful, it is inexpensive, and it is equally suitable for both sexes ... to be unable to swim is a discredit to a human being. It is positively humiliating to be at the mercy of a few feet of water, and no one can take his place as lord of creation when he can lose his life by falling into a pond or getting out of his depth when bathing.[13]

The notion that British men should be 'lords of creation' is a reflection of a contemporary idea which held that, if the British had a God-given right to rule over other less civilised nations, then the people in charge of the empire should strive for physical perfection. After the publication of Charles Darwin's *On the Origin of Species* (1859) some intellectuals incorporated aspects of Darwinian thought into their political philosophies. Walter Bagehot's *Physics and Politics* (1874) posited that, in international history, stronger and militarily advanced nations dominated weaker ones. Benjamin Kidd in *Social Evolution* (1894) and *Control of the Tropics* (1898) argued that the Anglo-Saxon 'race' was the 'master race'. The Anglo-Saxon race would only remain the master race, so it was reasoned, if its members were in peak physical condition.

The most disturbing branch of this Social Darwinist theory was put forward by Karl Pearson (1857–1936) who applauded the decimation of 'backward' indigenous societies and gloated about the fact that members of the Anglo-Saxon and Teutonic races had driven Native Americans from their land. However, Pearson's views were distasteful to many of even the most committed Victorian imperial ideologues. There was certainly a belief in British exceptionalism at the time. Many people did indeed believe that Europeans and the British in particular were in some way culturally, if not biologically, superior in some way to the indigenous peoples of the empire. There was likewise a belief that British racial superiority had to be maintained. Yet very few subscribed to the fundamentalist Social Darwinist theories espoused by the likes of Pearson.

The heroes of popular literature did not have to strictly be of British or Anglo-Saxon heritage. Those of northern European heritage were often viewed in just as positive a light as British heroes. Rider Haggard's *Eric Brighteyes*, for example, is the purported history of an Icelandic king named Eric (so-called Brighteyes because of his piercing blue eyes). In the preface, Haggard pointed out the affinity of race and culture between the English-speaking peoples and the 'heroic warriors' of northern Europe from the dark ages when he refers to '*our* Scandinavian ancestors'.[14] And Eric was portrayed as a tough and strong youngster:

> For he was strong and great of stature, his hair was yellow as gold, and his grey eyes shone with the light of swords … even as a lad his strength was the strength of two men; and there were none in all the quarter who could leap or swim or wrestle against Eric Brighteyes.[15]

The same type of admiration could be given, in a qualified manner, to Italians. G.A. Henty's *Out with Garibaldi* (1901) sees a young English lad called Frank called to assist Giuseppe Garibaldi in overthrowing the ruler of the Kingdom of the Two Sicilies, and in the process help to unify Italy.[16] Dreaming of military glory, he enthusiastically sets out for Italy.[17] While Garibaldi is the undisputed hero of the novel, Henty was clear that Italians were one rung below Englishmen on the racial ladder.[18] Under this hierarchy, the Germanic peoples were the master race. Underneath them were Latin people who were allegedly prone to idleness and effeminacy but whiter and above Asians and Africans. Henty

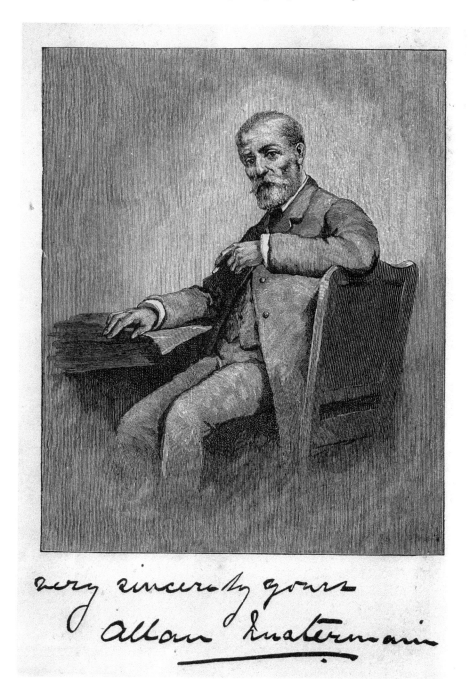

Intrepid explorer Allan Quatermain, the fictional star of several works written by H. Rider Haggard and the inspiration for Indiana Jones.

took inspiration for his Garibaldi novel from the true stories of around 600 Englishmen and Scotsmen who served as volunteers in Garibaldi's army and, according to a feature in the *Illustrated London News* in October 1860, left their country out of 'a love of adventure, as much, perhaps, as a love of freedom ... to fight for the liberty of a foreign people'. Henty's Garibaldi novel was still somewhat imperialist: young Frank's flying to the assistance of the Italians was still a projection of British power into a region in which the British had very few interests at stake and over which they did not rule.

Hunting was another means through which a British man might make himself lord of creation. Hunting was historically a pastime enjoyed by the British upper classes; since 1066, it was a jealously guarded right of the nobility. Anybody familiar with tales of Robin Hood will know that a common occurrence in retellings of the legend is the outlaw's defiance of authority by hunting the king's deer in the royal forests. In the early nineteenth century, hunting in England was still considered predominantly the preserve of the gentry and aristocracy. In the far-flung corners of the empire, however, it became an activity which British people from relatively humble stations in life could participate. Lord Roberts of Kandahar in his autobiography records that in the 1860s, even junior officers such as himself were permitted to enjoy the hunting season in Peshawar, and he continued to enjoy hunting until the very end of his career in India.[19] Virtually every late-Victorian imperial adventure story features a hunting episode. In Rider Haggard's *King Solomon's Mines* (1885), readers were first introduced to Allan Quatermain, who in the first chapter was laid up in bed with an injured leg. While the prospect of first encountering a hero laid up in bed is hardly an inspiring sight, readers soon learnt the reason why Quatermain was laid up:

I am laid up here at Durban with the pain in my left leg. Ever since that confounded lion got hold of me I have been liable to this trouble, and being rather bad just now, it makes me limp more than ever. There must be some poison in a lion's teeth, otherwise how is it that when your wounds are healed they break out again, generally, mark you, at the same time of year that you got your mauling? It is a hard thing when one has shot sixty-five lions and more, as I have in the course of my life, that the sixty-sixth should chew your leg like a quid of tobacco.[20]

Allan was not a public school boy but an ageing and rugged man who had led an active life. He learnt the basics of reading and writing – nothing too 'effeminate' – but spent most of his time since his youth engaged in various professions such as diamond mining and hunting big game.

Likewise, as an adult officer in the East India Company army, Charlie Marryat from *With Clive in India* demonstrates his manliness and bravery by hunting a tiger:

> Then the bushes were burst asunder, and the great yellow body hurled itself forward upon Charlie. The attack was so sudden and instantaneous that the latter had not even time to raise his rifle to his shoulder. Almost instinctively, however, he discharged both of the barrels; but was, at the same moment, hurled to the ground, where he lay crushed down by the weight of the tiger, whose hot breath he could feel on his face. He closed his eyes, only to open them again at the sound of a heavy blow, while a deluge of hot blood flowed over him … Charlie drank some brandy and water, which Hossein held to his lips. Then the latter raised him to his feet. Charlie felt his limbs and his ribs. He was bruised all over, but otherwise unhurt, the blood which covered him having flowed from the tiger.[21]

Other novels feature a variety of hunting scenes where the hero gets the better of a bear, a lion, a tiger, or even an elephant. The hunting of big game helped colonialists to develop several useful qualities: bravery, endurance, camaraderie, and marksmanship. While Quatermain's boast of having shot 'sixty-five lions and more' may seem like an exaggeration, in real life it was at the more modest end of British hunters' records. Sir John Hewitt, for example, shot over 150 tigers in India before his retirement in 1912. The numbers of animals shot by European colonialists often 'ran to excess', according to Stephen Mosley, and by the early 1900s sport hunters themselves were increasingly concerned about the dwindling numbers of big game stocks. This led to the signing of the Convention for the Preservation of Wild Animals, Birds, and Fish in

Drawn for this Magazine by

GEORGE HAWLEY.

"PLEASE, CAPTAIN,' SAID THE LITTLE CHAP, "MAY I GO BELOW TO PRAYERS ?"

An illustration from a Victorian boys' magazine illustrating the importance of Christian devotion which was impressed upon all would-be imperial servants through the pages of adventure fiction and short stories.

Africa in 1900, which sought to encourage colonial governments to place limits on hunting. It was not only over elements such as water that the British imperialist should make himself master but also over the animal kingdom.

Young soldiers' athletic abilities would serve them well not only while hunting but also more generally when it came to serving in harsh and inhospitable environments. There was a steady stream of articles in boys' periodicals and popular fiction in which the boy heroes had to be fit and tough to survive the searing heat of Africa or Australia or the snowy wilds of northern Canada. An article entitled 'Captain Sturt's Last Journey', which appeared in the *Young England Annual*, recounted the final exploration of the eponymous colonial administrator who, in 1844, set out with a party of explorers to chart the interior of New South Wales in Australia. This was a brave feat in view of the scorching heat which almost killed the adventurers. Had they not been fit and healthy, the article implies, they would most certainly have died. In the end, Sturt never actually accomplished his mission. Nevertheless, the excursion is presented in literary accounts as a victorious defeat: Sturt could have pressed on, and certainly possessed the ability to do so, but, ever attentive to the needs of those under his charge, he gallantly conceded defeat to the elements to spare the lives of his men.

Charlie Marryat in *With Clive in India* was slight of build but could run fast. Sometimes it served colonial adventurers better to be strong, as it does for Allan Quatermain in *King Solomon's Mines*. Allan and another two explorers venture into uncharted territory in Africa to rescue an associate who has gone missing. Their strength enables them to escape some hair-raising predicaments. As a reward for helping to overthrow the tyrannical ruler of the lost kingdom, Kwala, the explorers are promised access to the fabled mines of the Biblical King Solomon which are said to be full of treasures beyond men's wildest dreams. The mines are only accessible, however, by travelling through a series of deep caverns in the mountains which surround the lost kingdom. Yet their guide, a mad old woman named Gagool, who was the confidante of the deposed Kwala, betrays them; she does indeed lead them into the cavern of treasures but neglects to tell them that the minute they pick up any item the door will slam shut. Quatermain and his fellows find themselves trapped in the cavern. While the men have a few moments of panic, they soon calm down and ration out the last of the food and water. As luck would have it, Quatermain finds a trapdoor on the ground, with a heavy wrought iron ring around it to enable the door to be opened. It is almost too heavy for the explorers, but it is an obstacle which they can overcome if they all work as a team:

> "Heave! Heave! It's giving!" gasped Sir Henry; and I heard the muscles of his great back cracking. Suddenly there was a grating sound, then a rush of air, and we were all on our backs on the floor with a heavy flag-stone upon the top of us.[22]

It is the protagonists' strength which helps them in this fateful hour. Rider Haggard finished this passage by saying, 'never did muscular power stand a man in better stead'.

Quatermain was not particularly well-read but he knew parts of the Old Testament by heart. All good men of the empire were supposed to be good Christians. The development of pupils' physical health in the public schools was supposed to proceed in tandem with the improvement of their moral health. It was Arnold who originally posited the necessity for a strong religious component in educational instruction when he set about reforming Rugby School. In a letter to one of his associates he wrote that 'with regard to reforms at Rugby, give me credit, I must beg of you, for a most sincere desire to make it a place of Christian education. At the same time my object will be, if possible, to form Christian men.'[23] To this end, Arnold would deliver 'sermons', not lectures, to the lads in

DAVID LIVINGSTONE

Missionary and explorer, David Livingstone, whom the Victorians regarded as a hero of the empire because he fearlessly ventured into the so-called 'Dark Continent' to spread the banner of Christ and 'civilise' Africa.

Iillustration of the boat upon which David Livingstone sailed up the Zambezi River and into the so-called 'Dark Continent', a name given to Africa because its interior remained largely unexplored by Europeans.

the schools. He advocated a moderate system of corporal punishment – flogging – to teach the boys that he would never be wantonly cruel, but that they had to humbly submit to any punishment when they deserved it. When Arnold recruited new teachers, he had a clear sense of the type of man needed to instruct boys: 'what I want is a man who is a *Christian* and a gentleman, an *active* man, and one who has common sense and understands boys'.[24] The boys were to be active in both a physical and a spiritual sense: physical fitness would make them good soldiers but their Christian instruction would enable them to spread the gospel in the hostile environments to which they were sent.

The sense that young men should become soldiers of both Christ *and* the empire was promoted in popular literary works. Eva Hope described one of the most famous imperial warriors, General Charles Gordon (1833–85) as 'a true soldier of the Lord Jesus Christ'.[25] Gordon was what we might call an independent Christian; he did not profess an attachment to any particular denomination but maintained friendships with and respect for Roman Catholics, Methodists, Anglicans, and Presbyterians.

He imagined the theological world in purely military terms, viewing all Christian denominations as separate 'regiments' of Christianity as a whole. While Gordon's 'broad church' view of Christianity was uncommon, there was one journalist who, back in England, spoke in similar terms of the existence of a 'Church of the British Empire'. This idea, if fully realised, would accommodate various believers into one denomination. However, this idea never appears to have gained any currency among the various missionary bodies or even the public-at-large.[26]

It was not only the army and explorers that would benefit from athletic development and Christian instruction, or 'Muscular Christianity', for missionaries had to ensure that they were physically up-to-the-task of surviving in harsh environments. For the civilising mission to be fully realised, the 'savage' people of the colonies needed to be converted to Christianity.[27] A missionary such as David Livingstone could be lauded as a hero of the empire as much as any soldier. John Roberts wrote in 1870 that Livingstone was 'a truly great man ... a living lesson which the youth of our country cannot take too closely to heart'. His efforts in establishing three Christian missions in the 'dark continent' of Africa, furthermore, 'may be regarded as ... the fitting crown of his heroic and glorious career'.[28] Although not a military man, Livingstone's deeds at least equalled the heroism of any soldier. An anonymous writer in *Young England* expanded upon this idea by saying that

> [The missionary] goes out to plant the banner of Christ on hostile territory, or at all events, neutral territory. He is a scout and a pioneer, attacking force and army of occupation, all in one ... they go out on long tours through the country, sleeping on the floors of native houses, enduring the most severe physical fatigue, exposed now to great frosts, now to terrible summer heat.[29]

The importance of learning to swim is again highlighted in this article. The author says that 'when the rains come on, [missionaries] have to be ready to swim the rivers they cannot ford ... truly it needs a heroic heart to be a missionary'.[30] The British imperialist, be he soldier or missionary, had to make himself 'lord of creation', not only to serve the empire but to serve God as well.

Imperial adventurers could call on God in their hour of need. The colonial environment was dangerous for a number of reasons. If local populations were not hostile, there were diseases and dangerous animals with which to contend. Some fictional adventurers certainly got the better of lions and tigers. Lions were strong, ferocious, yet noble beasts, but they could be tamed and were relatively easy to kill, with a rifle at any rate. Often the animals were drugged by the Sahib's servants before the hunt began ('Sahib' was a term by which Indian servants addressed their British colonial masters). But there was one animal which often struck fear into the hearts of even the most resolute and brave adventurer: the serpent. Nevertheless, God was their protection, as related in *Heroes of the Empire* (1906) when two explorers are travelling through the jungle of an unspecified colony:

Livingstone was not the first explorer to make inroads into the interior of the African continent; Mungo Park also explored Africa in the late eighteenth century. Park's trip, however, was concerned with gathering scientific knowledge. Livingstone's mission was different: he wanted to explore but also to claim new territories for Christ.

"Lad," said Joe solemnly, "there is one deathbed repentance in the Bible, and only one, and I heard a good minister say that one was given us that none might presume and that none need despair."

"The words were hardly out of his mouth before I stood face to face with death! We had been tramping through a bit of marshy ground, and I was leading, when from the bough of a tree, like a flash of lightning, came the head of an enormous serpent.

"I stood paralysed, and then came Joe's voice from behind, clear and distinct: 'He is also able to save them to the uttermost that come unto God by Him,' and in that moment of dire extremity I gave myself to Christ forever … as I stood there, a wonderful thing happened. The snake uncoiled its huge body from the limb of the tree and glided away untouched."[31]

Many English readers might never have encountered a snake in real life. They were animals known chiefly through their representation as dangerous and deadly creatures in popular literature.[32] As the above passage shows, when faced with one of the most frightening animals and in the most dire predicament,[33] the brave colonialist could trust in God for deliverance, and he would be saved.[34]

Robert Baden-Powell inspecting sick horses during the Boer War. Baden-Powell wrote several works with a view to encouraging young men to be fit and healthy and ready, should the need arise, to serve the army. He went on to found the Scouts in the early 1900s. Image supplied with thanks to the Wellcome Library.

Hunting animals may have been a fine sport but exercise was promoted more generally because ultimately the British wanted tough soldiers to ensure they were victorious on the battlefield. According to an anonymous writer in *Peter Parley's Annual*, Robert Clive was a strong, physically fit young man and, as a result, there was no physical obstacle which he could not overcome; it was through his actions, of course, that the British found themselves masters of the subcontinent.[35] *The Boy's Own Paper*, in one of its many articles on fitness advice, sniped at overweight and bookish boys who would ultimately be of no use to the country in its hour of need:

> We always feel very sorry when we see in a crowd of restless youngsters the typical fat boy who, although perhaps only fourteen or fifteen, pulls the scale down at eleven stone or thereabouts; the sort of lad who lolls in the playground, looking out of his sleepy eyes and wondering what merit the other fellows can see in their games ... Fortunately for Old England, this is not usually the stuff of which her boys are made, the boys who in some time will be called upon to protect her shores or interests at home or across the seas.[36]

The association between sport and imperialism meant that in contemporary literary works the field of battle was presented as though it was a football match, as a poem from an 1865 issue of the *Radleian* reveals:

> A hero we may style
> The Chief in any game,
> A hero in a playful war,
> But a hero all the same.
>
> A hero who at football,
> All boldly meets the foe,
> And ever risking broken limbs,
> Still fear can never know.[37]

There was little in any of these literary works which made readers aware of the hardships, dangers, killing, maiming, and mental trauma involved in fighting in the front line. Warfare was instead depicted as a fun activity that was likened to a game. *The Boys of the Empire*, for example, referred to 'the Game of War'.[38] In Henty's *Tales of Daring and Danger* (1890), a young midshipman, after a naval battle against Chinese battleships in which many lives are lost, remarks: 'Has it not been fun!'[39] One of the most explicit depictions of war as a sport came in Robert Baden-Powell's *Sport in War* (1900):

> "What sort of sport did you have there?" is the question with which men have, as a rule, greeted one on return from the campaign in Rhodesia; and one could truthfully say, "We had excellent sport." For, in addition to the ordinary experiences included in that head, the work involved in the military operations was sufficiently sporting in itself to fill up a good measure of enjoyment.[40]

Baden-Powell served the empire in India and South Africa. He began his career as an army scout where he led reconnaissance missions. In the heat of a battle, he would survey the field, go behind enemy lines if necessary, and report back to his commanders on the other side's movements. A high level of physical fitness was required for this role and Baden-Powell made it all sound rather exciting:

> There was no drawing up of opposing forces in battle array, or majestic advancing of earth-shaking squadrons to the clash of arms; but you had to approach a koppie or peak of piled-up granite boulders, where not an enemy was visible, but which you knew was honeycombed with caves and crannies all full of watching niggers firing guns of every kind and calibre. You were expected to climb up this loop-holed pyramid to gain the entrance to its caves, which was somewhere near the top, and if you were lucky enough to escape an elephant bullet from one side or another, or a charge of slugs from a crevice underfoot, you had the privilege of firing a few shots down the drain-like entrance to the cave, and of then lowering yourself quickly into the black uncertainty below.[41]

Baden-Powell regretted that in the midst of the action he never appreciated these kind of tasks for the 'sport' that that they were. After all, being shot at by an enemy was just like a game – apparently – for there was a 'glorious uncertainty' about it.[42]

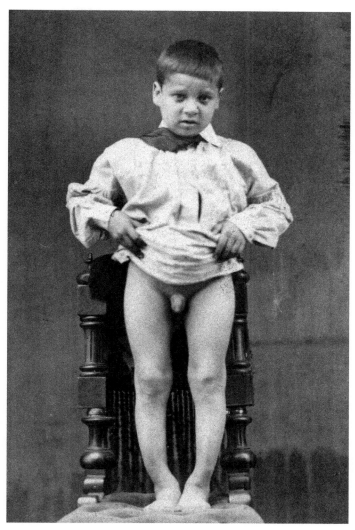

A photograph from the late-Victorian era showing a child suffering from rickets. This disease is caused by a Vitamin D deficiency. Its symptoms are the 'bow leg' and 'pigeon chest' look. Pollution was often so bad in the major Victorian cities that the smog blocked out the sun. One of the reasons why athleticism and physical fitness was promoted so widely in children's literature was because the working classes – the future rank and file of the imperial army – were unfit. A staggering number of working-class volunteers for the Boer War had to be turned away because they were not in peak physical shape, not only because of diseases like rickets but also because they were malnourished. Late-Victorian imperial ideologues feared that the British Empire would fall like Rome if its soldiers were unfit. Image supplied with thanks to both the London Science Museum and the Wellcome Library.

This illustration is taken from a book entitled *For School and Country*. The fit and healthy young protagonists always exercise in school and in their leisure time. They go on to become brave soldiers of the empire.

Baden–Powell rose through the ranks of the British army to become a commander. He became a national hero back in England due to his heroic conduct at Mafeking during the Second Boer War. When he returned to England in 1903, he published a children's edition of his book entitled *Aids to Scouting* (1899). It was a commercial success and its principles were adopted by both teachers and the leaders of youth organisations such as the Boys' Brigade, and in 1907 Baden-Powell established the Scouts movement. One reason for his book's success was the national concern over the nation's health. At the beginning of the Second Boer War, army recruiting officers found that many of working-class volunteers had to be rejected because they were unfit and often malnourished. George W. Steevens was alarmed at this perceived national degeneracy, but it was also unsurprising due to the working classes' poor living conditions:

> It would be difficult indeed to credit the full horrors exhibited by such districts as Lancashire or the Black Country at the end of the nineteenth century. There the wildest flights of hyperbole were equalled and exceeded by dismal truth, and the sun was literally obscured at noonday. A host of ungainly chimneys loaded the air with poisonous fumes which oppressed the hardiest species of vegetation. The inhabitants, penned up by day in close factories or the dimmer and more stifling obscurity of mines, herded by night in crowded tenements, were pale, sickly, and meagre … In sport, as in its analogue, war, the British degenerated with frightful rapidity.[43]

The working classes were not healthy. As well as being underfed, they lived in smog-filled cities which sometimes obscured the sun. This led to many children getting rickets, caused by a Vitamin D deficiency, leading to irregular bone growth and developing symptoms such as the 'pigeon chest' and 'bow legs'. If England's future working-class did not practice 'manly' exercises, elites feared that the British race would degenerate and that the country might lose its place as a world power. The British Empire could fall like all of the empires preceding her had done.[44] Athleticism was, therefore, promoted in the public schools but the ideology was subtly disseminated into popular literature and would, it was hoped, encourage those from outside the narrow middle-class ranks of the public schools to become fit and healthy soldiers. They would be ready to serve the British Empire in any capacity when called upon, and serve it as best they could. However, the literary heroes of the empire also knew that they had to be good sports. These characters were, for the most part, chivalrous and, in concert with their Christian beliefs, they had to be committed to the principle of fair play.

Chapter 4

For Right, for Freedom, for Fair Play!

Honour, courage, fortitude, and love of manly fair play; characteristics so strongly indented in the British character, that they are known and acknowledged from pole to pole.

Pierce Egan, *The Book of Sports* (1832)

The Liberal Empire stands in for world peace, for right, for freedom, for fair play. It is the great "Fair Play" Empire of the world.

The Lloyd George Liberal Magazine (1926)

It was all very well for young men to be brilliant athletes who could serve their country on the pitch and on the battlefield, but they needed to know that this in itself was not enough. Being a good imperial servant was also a matter of how a man conducted himself. One had to be a good sport as well as a Christian gentleman and a good athlete. The best men played by the rules on the pitch and on the battlefield. There were, in theory, rules to war just as there were rules for football: every fight should be a fair fight.

By the 1800s, many writers assumed that there was something uniquely *English* about the ideal of fair play in sport and war, and Englishness at this period was, to all intents and purposes, slowly becoming synonymous with Britishness. Pierce Egan the Elder in his *Book of Sports* (1832) made such an argument in his defence of pugilism.[1] In spite of its rather misleading title, *The Book of Sports* was a weekly periodical. In both *The Book of Sports* and his other magazine, *Boxiana*, Egan recounted numerous instances of athletes being good sports and treating their opponents with respect.[2] This 'manly love of fair play' in the boxing ring was just as applicable to the theatre of war because 'fair play is a Briton's motto' and British soldiers always treat their enemies well if they are ever captured as prisoners of war.[3] In fact, Egan argued that one of the reasons

A photograph from the 1920s of a boys from a public school playing a game of rugby. One of the reasons that the modern rules for games such as rugby, football, and cricket developed was because of the idea of fair play. It was all well and good for the public schools to allow boys to play sports, but when they were playing against other schools, they had to know how to play in a manner acceptable to the opposing team. The game had to be fair.

that Britons had abolished slavery was because of their innate sense of fairness, which they sought to extend to the ends of the earth.[4] That was of course a very patriotic, nationalistic, self-congratulatory idea of the concept of fair play. Egan neglected to mention that at the time that he was writing, the slave trade had indeed been abolished but slavery was still legal throughout the empire.

Many of the sports which Egan reported on in his magazines were only loosely regulated and often rowdy events. It was towards the second half of the nineteenth century that sports such as soccer were professionalised and clear rules governing their play were set down. This development came from the public schools. We noted previously that some of Arnold's reforms at Rugby allowed the pupils a degree of self-governance. One of the ways in which the pupils exercised this was to set down rules for their field sports which they considered fair, to ensure that everyone knew what was expected of them on the pitch. Pupils at Rugby in 1845 decided that it was permissible for players to handle the ball whereas pupils at Eton decided that it was not. The rules for a game similar to modern soccer were codified when representatives from Eton, Harrow, Rugby,

Winchester, and Shrewsbury met at Cambridge in 1849. They were then adapted and improved upon when the Football Association was formed in London in 1863, from when we can date the birth of modern soccer (from the abbreviation 'Assocer', for 'Association'). The codification of rules for sports such as tennis and cricket followed a similar process. All players should still play at their best to try to win the game, but they should never break the rules.

As the sports pitch was envisaged as a precursor to the battlefield, so imperialists took their sense of fair play out into the colonies, and the protagonists of Victorian literature were always depicted as having an innate love of fair play. Yet this did not emerge solely from the fact that a few public school boys decided to write some rules down for their football games. In their promotion of fair play in sport and battle, Victorian writers drew upon the twelfth-century ideal of chivalry. This entailed fighting an opponent in a fair and just manner, protecting women, and supporting righteous causes. Chivalric ideals were found in both the

Robin Hood meets his match, in an engraving by John Bewick completed in 1795. It was often thought by late-Victorian writers that there was something uniquely English about the ideal of fair play which stretched back to the medieval period. A common trope in retellings of the outlaw's legend was of Robin Hood meeting a man in the forest, having 'a fair fight' with the stranger, before shaking hands at the end and making friends.

courtly literature of the Middle Ages and also in more down-to-earth literature. Late medieval and early modern ballads of Robin Hood, for instance, often depict the eponymous outlaw in a Robin-Hood-meets-his-match scenario. Robin stops a stranger in the forest and the two of them proceed to have a fight with quarterstaffs. The stranger usually ends up winning the fight but Robin is good natured about it and the stranger is usually invited to join Robin Hood's band of merry men afterwards.[5] Some went so far as to argue that it was Robin Hood songs which fully represented 'the old English love of fair play and straight dealing'.[6]

Long periods of brutal war in the late medieval and early modern period made the idea of chivalry seem a bit ridiculous and playwrights such as William Shakespeare mocked its overly-romanticised ideals.[7] It was only in the late eighteenth and nineteenth centuries that chivalry was 'rediscovered', and many writers and cultural leaders became proponents of an adapted and reformed code of chivalry that could be practiced by men of all classes in their own period, resulting in a harmonious society.[8] Walter Scott's *Ivanhoe* (1819) did much to resurrect this contrived idea of chivalry which, theoretically, involved the working classes showing loyalty to the upper classes, with the upper classes looking out for the interests of those less fortunate. After the publication of Scott's book, as well as several poems inspired by the Middle Ages, the period was imagined as a time of jousting tournaments, of knights rescuing damsels-in-distress, and of crusaders gallantly going off to the Holy Land to defend Christendom in a just war. Most importantly, it was imagined as a time when soldiers from opposing sides treated their enemies with respect – Victorian historians had only to point to the legend which alleges that the Muslim ruler Saladin, upon learning that his enemy Richard the Lionheart was ill with a fever, sent a gift of some fruit to Richard to help him get better (there are a few variations on this legend: some say that Saladin sent an apothecary or emissary, and even a new horse at one point).

During the era of 'new' imperialism, the soldiers of the empire were often likened to medieval knights; the latter-day knights of the empire were supposedly just as committed to the ideal of fairness as their medieval forbears; men such as General Gordon, for instance, 'united all that is noble and chivalrous in a man', according to Eva Hope.[9] The

Crusades of the medieval period were depicted in Victorian literature as proto-imperialist endeavour, with chivalrous knights going off to fight for the advancement of Christendom and protecting the weak from the oppressed.[10] Newbolt summarised the late-Victorian neo-medieval ideal of chivalry in his *Book of the Happy Warrior* (1917): the idea was not to hate one's enemy but respect him while still endeavouring to win the day. A just war could be honourably conducted, therefore, if all warriors of the empire followed these principles.[11]

One did not have to be a member of the middle-class officer ranks to adhere to this revived form of chivalry because these tenets should be adhered to by people of all 'rank, creed, colour, or nationality'.[12] As an ideal, chivalry certainly had a wider application beyond the colonial battlefield, as Baden-Powell's *Scouting for Boys* (1908) illustrated, in which the rules of modern-day knights' conduct were laid down as follows:

1. Be Always Ready, with your armour on, except when you are taking your rest at night.
2. At whatever you are working try to win honour and a name for honesty.
3. Defend the poor and weak.
4. Help them that cannot defend themselves.
5. Do nothing to hurt or offend anyone else.
6. Be prepared to fight in the defence of your country.
7. Work for honour rather than profit.
8. Never break your promise.
9. Maintain the honour of your country with your life.
10. Rather die honest than live shamelessly.
11. Chivalry requireth that youth should be trained to perform the most laborious and humble offices with cheerfulness and grace and to do good unto others.[13]

Baden-Powell showed how even those in civil employments could be chivalrous and gentlemanly: 'a London policeman, for instance, is a gentleman, because he is well-disciplined, loyal, polite, brave, good-tempered, and helpful to women and children'.[14]

People from the East, especially those from the Arab and Muslim world, were often stereotyped in popular fiction as treacherous and ever-ready to betray their British allies.

Portrayals of British colonialists as fair-minded and chivalrous separated them from depictions of the 'savage' from the colonies, who were not to be trusted. In Captain Brereton's *With Roberts to Candahar* (1906) an officer declares that 'it is always a safe thing to suspect an Afghan ...

for they are treacherous as a nation'.[15] Eva Hope's biography of General Gordon describes him as 'loyal and true',[16] and towards the end of her history accuses virtually all of his Sudanese allies of treachery.[17] This was not conceived by English writers purely in terms of political treachery but also in Arabs' daily encounters with Europeans. H. Major's *Up the Nile* (1887) counselled readers that if they were to visit Egypt, then they should, if visiting a bazaar or marketplace, hide all signs of wealth, for the people there were not honourable and would attempt to extort more money from them.

For other writers after the middle of the century, an event known as 'The Black Hole of Calcutta' was the epitome of oriental treachery. During the Seven Years' War, Siraj Ud-Daulah captured Calcutta and promised his British captives, who numbered 146 souls, among whom were women as well, that he would spare their lives. However, that night Ud-Daulah's guards marched these prisoners into a prison cell that measured but 14 × 18 feet. In the searing Bengal heat this was a death sentence. F.M. Holmes in *Four Heroes of India* must have horrified younger readers when portraying the events of that night thus:

> Not even the most horrible torments of the Inquisition surpass the torments of that fearful night ... the windows of the prison were small and partly blocked; the torture of burning thirst, of stifling heat, and of the fearful lack of air became maddening. The seething mass of victims cried for pity, thundered at the doors, lost their reason, and fought and trampled on one another, while the fiendish guards held lights to the little windows, and laughed and jested at the fearful scene ... The fearful night wore itself away. Gradually the cries sank into the moans of the dying, and when the day dawned the fierce heat had already begun to decompose the dead bodies. Of the hundred and forty-six men and women driven into that dreadful den, one hundred and twenty-three were dead.[18]

Almost every late-Victorian book which referenced the Black Hole of Calcutta lays the blame for this treacherous act solely at Ud-Daulah's feet, although there is plenty of evidence to suggest that he did not order it and knew nothing about it until after the fact. No matter who ordered it, this was certainly not fair play.

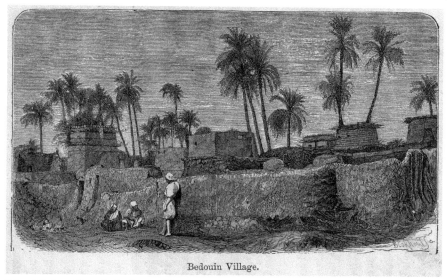

Bedouin Village.

The 'Oriental' and Arab world was stereotyped as backward and uncivilised. If Orientalist writers and artists were to be believed, the people of the East had hardly 'progressed' since Biblical times.

This depiction of native peoples as treacherous and cunning was part of the 'Orientalist' discourse which pervaded popular culture. The idea was first posited by Edward Said who argued that during the Georgian and Victorian periods, people from the imperialist West 'collected' knowledge about the East, or 'the Orient', and from this body of knowledge they formed racist stereotypes of the people and culture of the East which filtered down into popular culture. As we have seen, the East was viewed as an uncivilised and dangerous place. Paintings from the era show oriental towns and villages which seemed to have scarcely developed since Biblical times. The East was dangerous because of the diseases one could catch and the fearsome wildlife one might encounter. The people there were also held to be treacherous and often murderous. Oriental people, in Said's words, were stereotyped as 'gullible, devoid of energy and initiative, much given to fulsome flattery, intrigue, cunning'. In short, Muslims and Arabs, and those from the East more generally, were stereotyped as everything that the noble and chivalrous British race was not.

As an aside, it is important to note that Said's theories, while influential and useful for studying race relations throughout history, have been subjected to numerous criticisms. The most recent of these came from two scholars: Ibn Warraq and Daniel Martin Varisco. The general thrust of these scholars' arguments holds that, while there are merits to Said's work, it is much too generalised. The reason for this is that, when British and French politicians and scholars sought to understand the orient, its peoples and its cultures, this did not automatically come from a racist or white supremacist place as Said would have us believe. These scholars further argue that many prominent figures in the history of British and French imperialism actually admired the culture of the east, particularly in the eighteenth and early nineteenth centuries. We have indeed already encountered Warren Hastings's love for the Indian culture. Furthermore, while Said argued that imperialism was a peculiarly western idea, Varisco and Warraq point out that the people of eastern regions have engaged in imperialism with just as much gusto as western countries.

Part of an Englishman's innate sense of fairness required that the British unwaveringly supported their allies when called upon. Often in the schoolboy novels, a young boy could be seen defending a weaker lad from a bully, which is usually his first heroic and chivalrous act. An early scene in *From School to Battlefield* (1888) is fairly typical of these scenarios: a good lad called Harry vows vengeance on the school bully.[19] In depictions of peace and negotiations, British forces always promote both their own and their allies' interests equally. In *Forecastle Tom; or, Adventures by Land and Sea* (1884), a British naval captain, Tom, helps an indigenous tribe named the Caortians capture some Papuan pirates who have kidnapped a Caortian chief's fiancée. At the end of the battle a parley is held on the beach and Tom has this to say:

"I have but to say the word," exclaimed Tom, "and the fire-talkers will speak, and your men will be laid low."

"Speak on then."

"If you will quit the island peacefully and deliver over to my friend his promised wife," returned Tom, "we will permit you to go without further harm. Nay, since the Caortians are our allies, and have fought bravely on our behalf, you must also deliver up all their women whom you have taken prisoners."[20]

The Papuans decide not to take up Tom's terms which results in the death of them all:

> Akato [the Papuan villain] stood for a moment as if petrified with amazement. Then he burst into a loud laugh.
>
> "The white men are mad," he said; "let them go while there is yet time, or we shall drive them into the waters of the lake and drown them!"
>
> "You refuse then?"
>
> "Yes, yes!" cried Akato, shaking his spear impatiently.
>
> "Then you must abide by all that happens," cried Tom, "We will give you five minutes to consider."
>
> The reply was significant and characteristic. A javelin was hurled in perilous proximity to Tom's head. There was no need then for an order to fire. Every musket spoke. And amid a yell of despair the front line of savages fell, decimated.[21]

There is an obvious element of condescension in the manner which Tom speaks to the Papuans; his use of terms such as 'fire-talkers' to describe guns implies that the natives to whom he is speaking have the intellectual capacity of a child. The hurling of a javelin close to Tom's head after a parley has begun is a further instance of the stereotyping of non-Europeans as treacherous and cunning – negotiations are, after all, supposed to be entered into in good faith by both sides. While a modern reader might sympathise with Akato, to the Victorians, Tom would have been the most honourable one in the story: he had engaged with dialogue with the enemy and even given them a chance to escape with their lives while honouring his commitment to his allies, the Caortians.

The new chivalry had application also in civil society: encompassed within the notion of fair play was a commitment to *justice*, the parameters of which were widely defined. Sometimes it might mean 'justice' in a civil rather than a military sense, in the same way that Pierce Egan the Elder argued that the abolition of slavery stemmed from Englishmen's innate love of fair play. It could also mean ruling the natives fairly. Victorian biographers therefore praised men such as General Cornwallis, the Governor-General of India, who put an end to the abuses committed by East India Company

The fearsome ruler Ayesha, or, *She-Who-Must-Be-Obeyed*, sits in judgment over some of her rebellious subjects. She is a harsh ruler who, in order to maintain power, must exercise terror over her subjects, much to the dismay of the fair-minded English gentleman, Professor Holly.

officials who 'enriched themselves at the expense of the natives [...and] hunted out frauds of every kind'. Cornwallis's actions, so one Victorian writer surmised, made Company rule 'more acceptable to the natives'.[22] Trouble arose when colonial administrators ruled in an unjust manner, a point Henty recognised in *By Sheer Pluck* (1884), a story of the Anglo-Ashanti War of 1873–4. Before the war, in 1872, the British expanded their territory on the Gold Coast by purchasing a large portion of the region from the Dutch. Within the Dutch Gold Coast was a town called Elmina, which was claimed by the Ashanti king. The British and the Dutch, with the usual disregard they had for the wishes of the Africans, paid no heed to the claims of the Elminans or the Ashanti while negotiations were being carried out. The Ashanti then invaded Britain's new imperial acquisition when negotiations had finished. The British should have known better than to simply dismiss the Ashanti: the two powers had fought each other in 1823 as part of the second Anglo-

Ayesha in H. Rider Haggard's *She: A History of Adventure* was a highly sexualised woman capable of 'unmanning' her victims when she unveiled herself and allowed men to gaze upon her beauty.

Ashanti War, and the campaign was hardly a resounding victory for the British. The British were victorious in the war of 1873–74, and forced the Ashanti into a trade treaty and made them promise to end their practices of ritual human sacrifice. Yet Henty viewed this war as largely unnecessary: had the British only dealt with the people fairly, the war would never have happened. Henty laid the blame entirely at the feet of the British Empire's negotiators; the empire's representatives acted unfairly and their actions constituted a 'breach of faith' with the Africans.[23]

Explorers too had a sense of fairness and thought that the natives should be ruled in a just manner. Rider Haggard's *She* (1887) tells the story of Professor Holly and his adopted son, Leo Vincey. The pair embark on an expedition to find the lost kingdom of Kor in Africa because several old writings attest to the fact that Vincey is the reincarnation of the husband of an ancient ruler named Ayesha, or *She-Who-Must-Be-Obeyed*. Ayesha is a fearsome ruler. When Holly is brought before her, she makes him witness her sitting in judgement upon some of her citizens who have committed a crime:

> "Dogs and serpents," *She* began in a low voice that gradually gathered power as she went on, till the place rang with it … Ye have dared to disobey me … Hath it not been taught to you from childhood that the law of *She* is an ever fixed law, and that he who breaketh it shall perish? And is not my lightest word a law … ye have dared to disobey my word, this is the doom that I doom you to. That ye be taken to the cave of torture, and given over to the tormentors, and that on the going down of to-morrow's sun those of you who yet remain alive be slain.[24]

Rider Haggard fused the imperial gothic adventure genre with that of the late-Victorian travel narrative. He placed numerous footnotes throughout his novel which give it the air of being a factual, even scholarly account, of the two men's travels in the wilder parts of the world. This was the footnote which Rider Haggard placed under the scene of Ayesha's judgement:

> 'The cave of torture.' I afterwards saw this dreadful place, also a legacy from the prehistoric people who lived in Kor. The only objects in the cave itself were slabs of rock arranged in various positions to facilitate the operations of the torturers. Many of these slabs, which were of porous stone, were stained quite dark with the blood of the ancient victims that had soaked into them. Also in the centre of the room was a furnace, with a cavity wherein to heat the historic pot. But the most dreadful thing about the cave was that over each slab was a sculptured illustration of the appropriate torment being applied. These sculptures were so awful that I will not harrow the reader by attempting to describe them.[25]

The natives' crime was to attack Holly and Vincey on their approach to Ayesha's kingdom, when she had given express orders stating that no travellers should be attacked. Even though Holly was the victim of the natives' attack, he is disturbed at the disproportionate punishment which Ayesha intends to mete out to the poor natives, and he implores her to

ADMIRAL CORNWALLIS

From an engraving by BARTOLOZZI

General Cornwallis, a major figure in the American Revolution and who later served as the Governor-General of India. Image supplied with thanks to the Wellcome Library.

reconsider. Holly's entreaties on behalf of the condemned natives are to no avail as she responds that the only way to maintain her empire is through terror.[26] Her people, she says, are 'beasts' who need to be kept in check.[27] There will be no reprieve for the people who have disobeyed her, and they are condemned to a hideous death in the torture chamber.

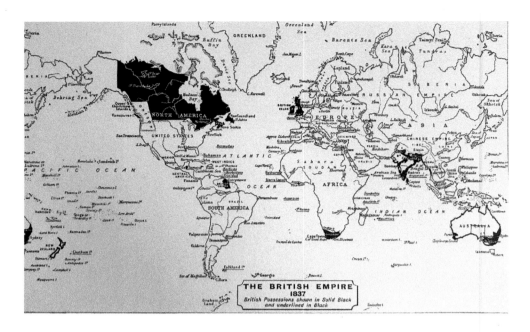

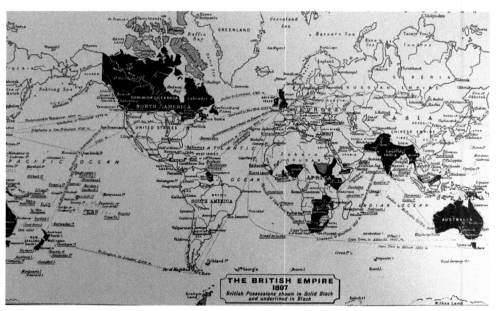

These maps highlight the extent of British imperial expansion at the beginning of Queen Victoria's reign and towards the end of it.

While so many of the texts studied in this book respond to imperial concerns, Rider Haggard was also reacting to concerns back home in Britain when he wrote *She*, particularly in regard to the emergence of the 'New Woman'. The New Woman was the nickname given to a certain type of woman who, from the 1880s, was free-spirited and throwing off the shackles of Victorian social expectations; she was usually well-educated and more interested in a career than in marriage and child-rearing. In a century in which women were thought by some medical professionals to have no sexual feeling, the New Woman pursued sexual enjoyment for its own sake. This was not just a British phenomenon but one which was occurring across Europe, and for many men this type of woman was a threat because it upset the social order. Ayesha is likewise a highly sexual and independent woman and has no problem revealing herself in full to Professor Holly.[28] Ayesha's tyrannical reign over her people is an example of when female independence could go too far. She has the power to metaphorically emasculate or 'unman' all those who look upon her face. While the men over whom she rules are only permitted to approach her throne by crawling on all fours, Holly – the quintessential Englishman – refuses to demean himself to a foreign ruler in such a way. Evidently the power that she possesses over others has gone to her head because she is incapable of ruling justly. The message in *She* then, is that had it been an Englishman ruling over these people, with a strong sense of fairness and justice, the poor natives would not have suffered as they did under the despot Ayesha.

The idea of fair play was not imperialist and stretched further back than the advent of new imperialism in the 1880s, but it took on a wider significance and often served to differentiate, in cultural terms at least, British soldiers from the supposedly devious and treacherous people whom they ruled. In practice, however, the ethos of 'fairness' on the battlefield was never fully reconciled with British imperialism in real life. This of course was the era when a Gatling or a maxim gun might be used against a tribe defending themselves with spears – hardly 'fair' in any sense of the word; the internment of women and children in concentration camps during the Boer War was likewise unchivalrous. Nevertheless, many Britons viewed it as their *duty* to rule over the people of far flung territories and 'civilize' them.

Chapter 5

Over the Hills and Far Away

Our 'prentice Tom may now refuse
To wipe his scoundrel Master's Shoes,
For now he's free to sing and play
Over the Hills and far away.
Over the Hills and O'er the Main,
To Flanders, Portugal and Spain,
The queen commands and we'll obey
Over the Hills and far away.
George Farquhar, *The Recruiting Officer* (1706)

"Of the record of such incidents of peril this book is full; but it is a part of a design to include some special reference to those cases in which peril has been encountered for the love of the fatherland, in the performance of duty, and the service of the country."
H.O. Arnold-Foster, *Peril and Patriotism* (1906)

"I have been learning a little of navigation. The first officer has been very kind to me, and I hope in the course of two or three years to pass and get a berth as a third mate. Still, I should like three or four years on board a man of war," [said Harry]. "I should think so," the old sailor said, "for a man ought to do his duty to his country … It is above all things essential, Harry, that you should do your duty."
G.A. Henty, *Do Your Duty* (c. 1906)

On 12 October 1799, Admiral Horatio Nelson arrived at Port Mahon, Minorca, on the *Foudroyant*. The purpose of his visit was to ask the island's governor to grant him some troops to assist him in his planned siege of Malta. While the ship was docked, Nelson also found time to write a brief autobiography. He presented himself as a 'self-made' man, and showed readers how he had been rewarded with titles and privileges because of hard work in his country's service. A life of service would serve readers well. 'Go thou and do likewise', Nelson urged them.[1] Yet one could not serve the nation purely in the hope of self-aggrandizement for there had to be a higher purpose; one should love and protect one's country and even be prepared to make the ultimate sacrifice in its defence.

Admiral Lord Viscount Nelson, the most famous naval hero of the Napoleonic Wars.

Almost six years to the day after Nelson wrote his autobiography, Great Britain was faced with the prospect of an invasion from Napoleonic France. On 21 October 1805, he stood on the deck of his flagship, *Victory*, with his fleet stationed off the coast of Cape Trafalgar, Spain. As the combined Franco-Spanish fleet approached the British force, Nelson, now Admiral

H.M.S. VICTORY, FIRST RATE, 104 GUNS, LYING IN PORTSMOUTH HARBOUR.

Admiral Nelson's flagship, HMS *Victory*.

Lord Viscount Nelson and commander of the fleet, ordered the following signal to be mounted: ENGLAND EXPECTS THAT EVERY MAN WILL DO HIS DUTY. This was a fight that the British could not afford to lose. Men had to do their duty. To do one's duty in battle, in service to the nation, was the highest form of patriotism. The British sailors present at Trafalgar had a *duty* to protect the nation and fight its enemies, even unto death.

The British fleet went on to a glorious victory at the Battle of Trafalgar and Napoleon's hopes of invading Britain were effectively destroyed. It would also be Nelson's last battle, for he was tragically wounded. A French sharpshooter on the *Redoubtable*, having come into close quarters with the *Victory*, shot a musket ball into Nelson's left shoulder which tore its way through his upper body and into his lower back. According to Robert Southey in *The Life of Nelson* (1813), the admiral died 'the most triumphant death … that of the martyred patriot … a hero in the hour of victory.'[2] Southey further mused on how the naval hero's life and death served as an example to others:

> He has left us, not indeed his mantle of inspiration, but a name and an example, which are at this hour inspiring thousands of the youth of England, – a name which will continue to be our shield and our strength.[3]

The whole nation was grateful to the heroic admiral who saved Britain from invasion. Nelson's praises were sung, not only by Southey in his book but, literally, in several popular street ballads of the day.

Although Nelson was admired as an imperial hero in late-Victorian writings, it will not have escaped readers' attention that, in the examples given above, there was very little said about the empire. The focus of patriotic feeling at this point was upon the British nation, which many contemporary writers equated solely with England. The empire rarely featured in popular patriotic literary works between the seventeenth and early nineteenth centuries. The popular song *Over the Hills and Far Away*, which first appeared in George Farquhar's *The Recruiting Officer* (1706), for example, focuses not upon imperial concerns but upon soldiers being sent wherever the monarch commands, and the theatres of war are listed as being Flanders, Portugal, and Spain, none of which were imperial possessions.[4] Reprints of the song on broadsides and in ballad collections were more concerned with giving England's old enemy the French, as well as the Spanish, a bloody nose, rather than supporting any explicitly imperial interests:

> Since now the *French* so low are brought,
> And Wealth and Honour's to be got,
> Who then behind wou'd sneaking stay?
> When o'er the Hills and far away;
> *Over the Hills, &c.*

> No more from sound of Drum retreat,
> While *Marlborough*, and *Gallaway* beat,
> The *French* and *Spaniards* every Day,
> When over the Hills and far away;
> *Over the Hills, &c.*[5]

This rather parochial focus upon the nation instead of the empire during the late eighteenth and early nineteenth century may seem strange. After all, this was the period of the great age of sail when Britannia (almost) ruled the waves. Yet the empire in contemporary patriotic writings was largely conspicuous by its absence.

Two things should be remembered: the first is that the empire was still being expanded primarily through the efforts of private trading companies. Nabobs like Robert Clive were hardly well-liked and received much censure in the press. In 1772 the government opened an inquiry into the East India Company's practices. Clive was one of the inquiry's targets with much of the criticism levelled against him being because of the vast sums of wealth he accrued while in India. James Mill in his history of India deplored the fact that the Company had been transformed from a commercial entity into a governing power and blamed Clive for corrupting the Company's original mandate for trade. Warren Hastings was actually impeached by the government when he returned to Britain on the grounds of mismanagement and the pursuit of unnecessary and costly wars against Indian states, although the charges were never

The ultimate sacrifice – the Death of Lord Nelson at the Battle of Trafalgar. Image supplied with thanks to the Wellcome Library.

substantiated and the trials fizzled out after a couple of years. It was not until the Victorian period that Clive's and Hastings's reputations received a posthumous rehabilitation in popular literature.[6]

Secondly, for early nineteenth-century writers, the most recent colonial war waged by the British state, the American War of Independence, was not one to celebrate, because Britain had lost colonies. Some in Britain were hostile the colonists' cause: Samuel Johnson, to take one example, was on the side of the government and declared that 'if the subject refuses to obey, it is the duty of authority to use compulsion'.[7] When news reached England of the colonists' defeat at Long Island in 1776, people in Leeds, Manchester, Bristol, York, and Halifax celebrated in the streets and burnt effigies of George Washington, John Adams, and John Hancock. In spite of this, public opinion in Britain towards the American war was mainly one of regret. Traders and merchants worried about how the unrest in the colonies would harm their trade, as in the following petition from Bristol Merchants written to the king in 1775:

It is with an affliction not to be expressed and with the most anxious apprehensions for ourselves and our posterity that we behold the growing distractions in America threaten, unless prevented by the timely interposition of your Majesty's Wisdom and Goodness, nothing less than a lasting and ruinous Civil War ... We are apprehensive that if the present measures are adhered to, a total alienation of the affections of our fellow subjects in the colonies will ensue.[8]

The idea that the war between the American colonies and Britain was a transatlantic 'civil war' was fairly widespread. Major John Cartwright (1740–1824), a naval captain and a democrat, who had served in the Seven Years' War and played a leading role in the Capture of Cherbourg and the Battle of Quiberon Bay, refused a commission to command a vessel which would be forced to fight against the American colonists. In a letter to Lord Howe (1726–99), Cartwright wrote,

Thinking as I do on the most unhappy contest between this kingdom and her colonies, it would be a desertion from my principles (which I am sure your Lordship would not approve of) were I to put myself in a situation that might probably cause me to act a hostile part against them.[9]

Back in Britain, when he was older, Cartwright became one of the most famous radical thinkers of the early nineteenth century, and wrote a series of pamphlets advocating universal suffrage, which was to even include women. Additionally, one British merchant navy captain, named John Paul Jones (1747–92), actually defected from the British side and joined with the Thirteen Colonies, and he was given command of several ships in the Continental Navy. Clearly when it came to feeling a sense of duty to the nation and empire in the context of the American War, the British people were conflicted.

This is not to say that the empire *never* figured in ideas of patriotism during the late eighteenth and early nineteenth centuries. Phebe Gibbs briefly conflated the East India Company with the British monarchy in *Hartly House*.[10] Yet popular patriotism focused more on giving the

Major John Cartwright, naval captain and radical. Many people in Britain objected to their government's handling of the crisis in America during the 1760s and 1770s. When tensions spilled over into a fully-fledged war between Britain and her thirteen American colonies, some naval captains such as Cartwright refused a commission to serve in what they saw as an unjust war. He later went on to become a political activist who advocated a number of progressive and radical causes. He was honoured with the erection of a statue to his memory in 1831, in the middle of what is now Cartwright Gardens, Bloomsbury. The inscription reads that he was 'a Firm, Consistent, & Persevering Advocate of Universal Suffrage, Equal Representation, Vote by Ballot, and Annual Parliaments. He was the first English Writer who openly maintained the Independence of the United States of America ... yet he nobly refused to draw his Sword against the Rising Liberties of an oppressed and struggling People.'

French a good hiding rather than celebrating imperialism. During the Seven Years' War, the British public enthusiastically celebrated news of the country's military successes overseas. It was Britons' intense dislike of Catholic France which was a strong unifying factor in the forging of British national identity when the nation was quite a new creation. When newspapers in the 1750s praised militiamen for enlisting, for example, they were lauded for doing their 'duty to themselves, their King and Country and … securing our religion, liberties, and properties from French tyranny and oppression.'[11]

The focus for British writers, artists, and intellectuals was more often than not upon fostering a sense of British *national* identity rather than an international imperial identity. In a comparatively short length of time, after all, four nations – England, Wales, Scotland, and Ireland – had been united into one kingdom. Britishness, so argues Linda Colley, was a 'top down' idea foisted by the intellectual and artistic elites of the new British state onto the people-at-large in its constituent nations. The late-eighteenth-century wars against the French, culminating in the French Revolutionary and Napoleonic Wars, occurred at the height of the Romantic Movement. Romanticism – an intellectual, literary, and artistic movement – emphasised individual imagination, emotion, and freedom. One reason why Romanticism became so popular with writers was because it was a reaction against the formalism and rigidity of neoclassicism, which originated on the continent and, in a word, it was not French.[12] Through their art, Romanticists were inspired to reconnect with and 'rediscover' their own national past, and in this endeavour they increasingly turned to Britain's medieval past. In the eighteenth century, historical research into Old and Middle English culture and folklore, as well as that of Scotland and Wales, was conducted by antiquaries; as a result of their efforts, in the nineteenth century there was a 'medieval revival' in English popular culture, spearheaded by the Romantics.

A notable instance of the British public's new-found love for their medieval past was the phenomenal success of Walter Scott's *Ivanhoe*. The novel was a piece of pure medieval spectacle featuring an 'all-star cast' of characters including Richard the Lionheart, Robin Hood and Prince John. Yet far from endorsing Richard the Lionheart's crusade in the Holy Land, Scott criticises such foreign adventures because they distract the

The ideology of bourgeois domesticity at its height, an ideal which even Queen Victoria and her family sought to convey in their public image, encapsulated here in Franz Xaver Winterhalter's painting of the Royal Family, completed in 1846.

king from social and economic problems at home, and overseas exploits usually divert his attention away from ongoing political corruption at the heart of the British establishment. As Southey's biography of Nelson made clear, then, a good patriot had to be loyal to the *nation* but not necessarily to the empire, and in turn, as Scott's work highlighted, good rulers would concentrate their efforts on ensuring the prosperity of their citizens.

Even into the mid-Victorian period, the focus of patriotism was England, and a military life was regarded by some as incompatible with what was then a very different standard of masculinity. For a man to be 'manly' in the early to mid-nineteenth century, he was expected to adhere to a bourgeois ideal of family life in which his care and attention was to be focused upon the home and he was to take responsibility for the protection of his family. He represented his family in public, while the wife's place was in the domestic sphere. As John Tosh notes, 'the home was central to masculinity, as the place where the boy was disciplined and the man attained full status as a householder.' The middle classes in the mid-Victorian era were the most powerful social group in economic, political, and cultural terms. Their adherence to this domestic ideal signalled their moral superiority over both the aristocracy and the working classes. The middle-class Victorian man was supposed to be different to the profligate nobleman who spent his nights on the town, neglecting his wife and committing adultery. By allowing his wife to remain at home and manage the household while he was the breadwinner, he could differentiate himself from the working-class man whose family members were compelled to work from necessity. Through such familial arrangements the middle-class male householder signalled to the world that he was of sound social and financial status. If he achieved those things then the family would be, in a word, 'respectable' – one of the moralist buzzwords of the age – and every self-respecting middle-class Victorian family aimed to be seen as respectable. It was a model of family life which Queen Victoria and Prince Albert sought to promote in their public image, an ideal most famously captured in Franz Xaver Winterhalter's impressive portrait of the Royal Family of 1846. The bourgeois Victorian householder certainly did not go gallivanting off to foreign climes. This did not mean, of course, that Englishmen did not love their country and that they were unaware or uncaring about what happened out there in the empire – we have already encountered Dickens's remarks on the Indian Mutiny – nevertheless, these factors, combined with the fact that artists and intellectuals were 'rediscovering' their national heritage, go some way to explaining why the empire was often of little consequence in ideals of duty and patriotism.

There was another author who did appropriate colonial settings frequently and extensively: William Makepeace Thackeray (1811–63). One interesting although not commercially successful novel of his was *The Virginians: A Tale of the Last Century* (1857–59), which is the story of how one family – hints of domesticity coming through here – deals with an imminent war. The novel, set during the lead-up to the American War of Independence, sees two members of the Warrington family, Henry and George, take opposite sides. Ultimately, George, the British officer, resigns his commission in the British army rather than take up arms against his sibling. Clearly Thackeray's message was that family should come before the empire.

In other Thackeray novels, readers might not have approved of his protagonists' motives for enlisting; they are by no means as noble and patriotic as those characters from later Victorian fiction. One of Thackeray's most famous novels, *The Luck of Barry Lyndon* (1844), tells the life story of the title character. He is depicted as a typical eighteenth-century rake – an immoral, womanizing man, of aristocratic descent, and usually in debt because of a gambling addiction. Lyndon, having realised that his prospects of marrying a rich heiress are slim, falls into bad company and his debts spiral. To escape his creditors, he enlists in the army to serve in the Seven Years' War. *Barry Lyndon* was similar to a *picaresque* novel. This term comes from the Spanish *picaro*, meaning 'rogue', a genre which first emerged in Spain in the sixteenth century. In such works, the protagonist recounts a series of adventures or misfortunes which befall him; he serves different masters, falls in with shady characters of the criminal underworld, and perhaps attempts to hatch some hare-brained scheme to make money until he is finally caught by the authorities and punished. Readers would have expected Lyndon to mend his ways at the end and assume his proper status as a married man and householder, which indeed he does towards the end of the novel, and he is even elected as an MP. Yet Thackeray liked to play around with his readers' expectations: Lyndon falls into his old ways again, visiting taverns and drinking houses, and spends the last nineteen years of his life in a debtors' prison.

If the idealised middle-class male householder was required to focus his attention on the home and family, it is natural to wonder how tales of heroes serving out in the colonies, many of whom did not have a family or whose families feature to only a limited degree in literary works, fitted around social and cultural expectations of manly domesticity. As we noted previously, the publication of Kingsley's *Westward Ho* really was a watershed moment, not simply because it was the first novel to explicitly

Sir Francis Drake who, according to (a most likely untrue) legend, was calm and collected in the face of danger, so much so that he insisted on finishing his game of bowls on Plymouth Hoe even though the Spanish Armada was approaching. Drake went on to have a 'starring role' in many late-Victorian popular fiction novels and was regarded by people in the nineteenth century as one of the heroes of the empire. Image supplied with thanks to the Wellcome Library.

turn its attention to imperial affairs, but also because we see a young lad of schoolboy age *enthusiastically* want to serve abroad to advance Britain's interests at the expense of foreign nations.[13] At the same time, as most of these books detailing imperialists' lives were being published in the mid-to-late Victorian era, society's perceptions as to what the proper duties of a man were began to change. As John Tosh further notes, there was a 'flight from domesticity'. Too much time spent at home, in the society of women, was thought to be 'unmanly'. In Kipling's *The Light that Failed* (1890), the man who drank tea with the ladies at 5.00pm was deemed to be effeminate. The middle-aged lower-middle-class man who secured himself a moderately salaried job as a clerk in the city and was attentive to his family's needs became the butt of satirists' jokes, a case in point being George and Wheedon Grossmith's *The Diary of a Nobody* (1892). Men needed time away from women to make them into men, to make them 'manly', and what better way to spend this time than in the country's service? Doing so would toughen them up and ensure that they were taking their proper place among the 'lords of creation'. 'Domesticity', as Tosh further notes, 'was therefore at odds with the values espoused by the public schools.'

A young man, by the latter part of the Victorian era, should want to do his duty to his Queen, country, *and* empire. This was the mentality fostered ever since sports became a prominent part of the public school curriculum and filtered down into popular literature. There was a natural progression from being loyal to one's captain on the pitch and dutifully serving the monarch and empire, as Baden-Powell counselled the lads of Cottesmore School in Brighton in 1900.[14] Other writers echoed Baden-Powell's sentiments, stating that one should always be ready to serve ones team captain and do what he asks without a murmur, for this was a quality that would be useful to the nation when a man was called to serve.[15] British soldiers could only carry out their duties effectively if they remained calm under pressure on the battlefield even when faced with seemingly insurmountable odds. It is no surprise that the apocryphal story of Sir Francis Drake continuing to play bowls on Plymouth Hoe even after he had been warned that Spanish ships were approaching, gained new currency in late-Victorian literature as exemplifying the calm and collected attitude of Englishmen before a battle, an episode which was related by Alfred Noyes:

The fleet of Spain had won the channel without a blow.
All eyes were turned on Drake as he stood there
A giant against the sunset and the sea
Looming, alone. Far off, the first white star
Gleamed in a rosy space of heaven. He tossed
A grim black ball i'the lustrous air and laughed, –
"Come, lads," he said, "we've time to finish the game!"[16]

Other military heroes were depicted as cool-headed, calm and resolute in the face of danger. In a biography of the Duke of Wellington, G.R. Gleig described Napoleon's conqueror thus: 'he is described by such as had the best means of observation, to have been calm, self-possessed, and cheerful throughout'.[17] It was often the calm and resolute nature of the British soldier or sailor which, in popular literary works enabled them to win a battle against all odds, as Henty implied in *With the Allies to Pekin* (1900).[18]

However, not every literary imperial hero performed their duties without complaining, as Baden-Powell had counselled. Ernest Foster's *Heroes of the Indian Empire* retells the story of Robert Clive's career in India, but he is headstrong, hot-headed, and bold:

One day, when he had allowed himself to be irritated by some duty which he was called upon to perform, he so grossly insulted one of his superior officers that he was commanded by the governor of the settlement to apologise.[19]

According to Foster, Clive felt humiliated by the apology he was reluctantly forced to make. The officer, wanting to make amends with Clive afterwards, then invited him to dinner, and was surprised when Clive refused his invitations, behaviour which would have been totally out-of-sync with the idealised ethos of the public schools: "No, sir," was the scornful answer; "the Governor desired me to apologise, and I have done so; but he did not command me to dine with you!"[20] Nevertheless, this was just a case of 'boys being boys'. Clive's youthful peccadilloes were cancelled out by the fact that he had a heroic and 'glorious career' which resulted in the East India Company gaining sovereignty over the subcontinent.[21]

It may have been hard for people in late eighteenth- and early nineteenth-century Britain to feel any great love or warm patriotic feeling for trading corporations such as the East India Company. Yet during the late-Victorian era, those same trading companies do become a focus for patriotism in literary works. The young Charlie Marryat in Henty's *With Clive in India*, before he sets out to take up the position of a writer in the East India Company, is told by his uncle that he must 'be steady and do your duty to your employers'.[22] The 'employer' in this case is the East India Company, hence duty to his employer is duty to the empire. There was another method by which Henty in his works tried to fire a zeal for the empire among his young readers. This was to ask them indirect thought-provoking questions. After some years serving in India, having gained the status of a 'sahib', Charlie returns to England with an Indian servant named Hossein:

Hossein was astonished at the multitude of white people, and inquired of Charlie why, when there were so many men, [had] England sent so few soldiers to fight for her in India; and for once, Charlie was unable to give a satisfactory reply.

"It does seem strange," he said ... "that when such mighty interests were at stake, a body of even ten thousand troops could not have been raised and sent out. Such a force would have decided the struggle at once, and in three months the great possessions which have cost the Company twelve years' war, would have been at their feet. It would not have cost them more, indeed, nothing like as much as it now has done, nor one tithe the loss of life. Somehow England always seems to make war in driblets.[23]

The 'mighty interests' at stake in the novel were the existence of the East India Company and of the fledgling Indian empire itself. Henty's remark about England always making war in driblets would have had special urgency for Henty; this was a time when Britain faced international rivalry for supremacy from the newly-unified Germany and the United States, Henty was exhorting younger readers to sign up to serve the empire, and to ensure that it lasted.

Of course, when authors were writing about someone else, and particularly when they had an imperialist message to impart to readers, their stories were often simplistic and contained the following message: service to the empire was a good thing and everyone wanted to do their part in whatever small way they could. There were some former soldiers, however, who in their autobiographies presented a more nuanced and realistic account of what it was like for a young man setting off from England to serve in the colonies. The autobiography of Lord Roberts of Kandahar entitled *Forty-One Years in India* gives us a glimpse into what it must have been like for many a young soldier setting out for India during this period:

> Forty years ago the departure of a cadet for India was a much more serious affair than it is at present. Under the regulations then in force, leave, except on medical certificate, could only be obtained once during the whole of an officer's service, and ten years had to be spent before that leave was taken. Small wonder, then, that I felt as if I were bidding England farewell forever ... My ship was the Peninsular and Oriental Company's steamer Ripon, commanded by Captain Moresby, an ex-officer of the Indian navy, in which he had earned distinction by his survey of the Red Sea. A few Addiscombe friends were on board, leaving England under the same depressing circumstances as myself, and what with wind and weather, and the thought that at best we were bidding farewell to home and relations for ten long years, we were anything but a cheerful party for the first few days of the voyage.[24]

Roberts was a celebrity in his own lifetime and, even while still alive, was cast as the hero of short stories in magazines such as *Chums*.[25] Although Roberts's 'youthful spirits' soon reasserted themselves, it was evidently a daunting prospect to leave England and was certainly not the excited attitude that young Charlie displays in Henty's *With Clive in India*.

One did not have to be a soldier of the empire to serve it. Some literary works depict clerks as dutifully performing a necessary, although at times monotonous, job to keep the empire administered effectively. In R.M. Ballantyne's *The Young Fur Traders* (1856), the men who work for

Field Marshall Lord Roberts of Kandahar rose through the ranks of the British army, from a mere subaltern to its Commander-in-Chief. He became something of a legend in his own lifetime, with novels written about him, and regularly appearing in illustrations for the popular Victorian satirical magazine, *Punch*. This image was the frontispiece to his best-selling autobiography: *Forty-One Years in India* (1897).

the Hudson's Bay Company in Upper Canada in the early nineteenth century do not live the life of Robinson Crusoe, as the young protagonist Charley wishes to, but loyally and quietly perform their duties to their employer.[26] The skills of the humble civil servant were just as necessary and valuable to the empire as those possessed by the soldier or the missionary. After all, was it not with just over 1,000 civil servants that the British were able to govern the Indian subcontinent containing over 300 million people? The important function of those in the imperial civil service was stated more explicitly in *Peril and Patriotism* (1906), in which the MP, H.O. Arnold-Foster, stated:

Queen Victoria became Empress of India in 1876.

> It is the glory of the Indian services, not that they have sent forth a few great, but that they have diffused over the country so many good, public officers, eager to do their duty … the whole body of public servants, each in his degree, and in accordance with his opportunities, may truly serve their country; and in so far as the least important of our public servants does his best work without fear or favour, without the stimulus of applause, or the hope of a special reward, because he desires to do his duty to his country, he is a true patriot.[27]

Arnold-Foster was probably blowing his own trumpet. Here was a man who was educated at Rugby, then at Oxford, and continued in 'white collar' occupations throughout his whole life. He served as the private secretary to his adoptive father, William Edward Foster, Chief Secretary for Ireland, and from 1884 Arnold-Foster was Secretary for the Imperial Federation League. When he was eventually elected as the Liberal MP for West Belfast, he was appointed as the Chief Secretary to the Admiralty.

He was also the author of several books and policy papers. His career was not the 'glorious' record of military victories enjoyed by a man such as Lord Roberts, yet the empire needed a man like Arnold-Foster all the same. The British Empire was like a machine in which each person was a cog; all of the constituent parts were necessary to ensure its smooth running.

The message in late-Victorian literature that was regurgitated time and again was this: when young lads grew up and became soldiers or servants of the empire, they should never shirk their duties towards their commanding officer, their country, their empire, and their Queen. At this time, Victoria herself was conceived not simply as a British monarch, as she had been in the earlier part of her reign, but rather as an imperial ruler. From the 1870s onwards, she was more often than not styled *Victoria Regina et Imperatrix*, having been granted the title of Empress of India by Benjamin Disraeli's Conservative government in 1876. Commemorative souvenirs manufactured for Victoria's Diamond Jubilee in 1897 likewise often referred to her as 'Queen and Empress'. The jubilee itself was, as Andrew Thompson notes, no event of mere national significance but one of international, imperial importance. The attendance of representatives from the dominions and colonies, all of whom paid homage to the empress, symbolised Victoria's role as the Queen of the United Kingdom and the forward march of British civilisation around the world. David Campbell's *Victoria: Queen and Empress* (1901) described the events of the jubilee:

> A new people, as it were, came to the front of the scene; and, added to the acclamations of her home subjects, were those of the vast throngs from pendent countries, who flocked from the remote corners of the world, glad of the opportunity to manifest their loyalty to a Queen, whom most of them had never seen, but had long and gladly known, through the medium of her far-reaching influence for the consolidation of all her peoples. Here marched in strong companionship the British regular and the Colonial horseman, the swarthy Asiatic and the eager African, men who were ready to lay down their lives for that vast Empire which the great imperial procession symbolised in all its splendour.[28]

The warm words of 'strong companionship' between the mother country and her subject peoples, of course, masked the growing calls from many quarters of the empire for either Dominion status, home rule, or full independence. Nevertheless, this was an empire which, so Campbell proclaimed, people should be prepared to pay the ultimate price. Given Britain's many and often now forgotten colonial wars, there was certainly no shortage of opportunity for a British soldier to die on the field of battle.

One famous general who paid the highest price for doing his duty was General Gordon. Eva Hope depicted him as a man who always dutifully carried out any task asked of him, even when what was asked of him 'was not all according to his wish'.[29] His first assignment as a young officer was the building of sea fortifications in Milford Haven.

"NEW CROWNS FOR OLD ONES!"

Queen Victoria in later life, no longer simply *Victoria Regina* (VR) but *Victoria Regina et Imperatrix* (VRI), 'Victoria Queen and Empress'.

Conservative Prime Minister Benjamin Disraeli who purchased a majority of the shares in the Suez Canal in 1875 after the Khedive of Egypt had gone bankrupt. Disraeli thereby ensured that Britain had safe and relatively quick passage to India: the jewel in the empire's crown.

This small Welsh coastal town may not have offered the young warrior any excitement but he did it without complaining. He soon got his wish to see some action when he was assigned to serve in the Crimean War in 1855, tasked with building trenches for the soldiers at Balaklava. Gordon is an interesting example because while he participated in many famous overseas campaigns, his imperial martyrdom occurred because he actually disobeyed orders from the government. Since 1819, Sudan had been under Egyptian rule, a country which was under the dominion of the Ottoman Empire. In the wake of a nationalist rebellion in Egypt in 1882, British and French forces, motivated by a need to ensure continued control of the Suez Canal, sent warships to Egypt in the hope of quelling the uprising. Some skirmishes occurred between the Egyptian army and the combined Franco-British forces but the Egyptians were defeated. The Egyptian government was then reinforced with British support, and Egypt became a protectorate of the British Empire, with Egyptian government policy overseen by British administrators.

When the British first assumed control of Egypt as a protectorate, the latter's finances were in a parlous state. Although Sudan was under Egyptian control, it was hardly cost-effective for Egyptian rule to continue over the region. Besides, Sudan was in the throes of a nationalist rebellion, led by a religious fundamentalist, Muhammad Ahmad (1844–85), who named himself 'The Mahdi' (the Guided One'). The Mahdi encouraged people to rise up and overthrow their Egyptian rulers. British colonial administrators simply did not want the headache of having to deal with a religiously-inspired rebellion that would be difficult to put down in a region which was, on the face of it, not worth the hassle of keeping. The British government decided that the Egyptian and European citizens stationed in Khartoum, Sudan's capital, should be evacuated. Gordon was chosen for this task, although some people in high places back in London had their doubts about his suitability for the role. As Gordon made his way through Sudan he began to be convinced that it was his godly duty, not only to evacuate the Egyptian and European inhabitants living there, but also, in Niall Ferguson's words, to 'smash up the Mahdi' and his forces.

Gordon's actions were in direct defiance of what the Liberal Prime Minister, William Gladstone (1809–98), had commanded. At this

George W. Joy's painting of *The Death of General Gordon* completed in 1885. Gordon was a Christian zealot who, in spite of having been ordered to simply evacuate Egyptian and European citizens from Sudan, decided instead to disobey his orders and hold the town of Khartoum and prevent the leader of the rebellious Mahdi from taking the town. Gordon held out for about a year, yet Prime Minister William Gladstone refused to authorise a relief mission. Eventually the town fell to the Mahdi's forces and Gordon was hacked to pieces. This image was reproduced in *Peril and Patriotism* (1906) and the original is in Leeds Art Gallery.

point in his political career, Gladstone was opposed to further imperial expansion. He had opposed Disraeli's original purchase of shares in the Suez Canal in 1875, and was highly critical of the popular imperialism promoted by the Tories. Indeed it was Gladstone who first used the word 'imperialism' to describe *aggressive* overseas expansion. However, Gordon thought that he knew best: Khartoum was a town which should be held at all costs. He was soon besieged by the Mahdi's forces, yet Gladstone refused to authorise sending a relief force, leading Eva Hope to declare that Gordon was

> Forsaken by the government ... in both Houses of Parliament questions in reference to the General's safety were repeatedly asked; but they were, as a rule, treated very lightly. Lord Granville declared that if General Gordon felt himself abandoned, it was because he had not received the government telegrams. Mr Gladstone said that the General was at liberty to leave Khartoum if he pleased.[30]

Gordon did not leave – he held the city of Khartoum for 313 days when the Mahdi at last broke through its defences, hacked Gordon to pieces and had his head placed on a spike. Yet far from blaming Gordon for his own overreach, in Eva Hope's biography the government was to blame, 'on whom will rest the bloodguiltiness for all lives hereafter lost in the Sudan'.[31] Gordon was 'the brave one' standing up for right over might. Hope was not the only person who thought this way; the public seemed overwhelmed with grief that one of its most famous Christian soldiers was dead at the hands of unruly 'savages', whose murderous act had been aided and abetted by an uncaring government. Gordon's last moments were immortalised in a painting by George William Joy, *General Gordon's Last Stand* (1893), in which Gordon stands proud and ready to meet his death like a true warrior. Below him the attacking forces are frozen in awe at the sight of him.

It was Egypt's parlous financial state that caused the British to abandon the Sudan. Yet they still believed that they had a moral right to rule over the region. When Egypt's economy had recovered by 1896, the Marquess of Salisbury's Conservative government deemed it expedient to reconquer Sudan and avenge Gordon's death. Besides, Ethiopia's recent

From *Harper's Magazine*.]   Copyright, 1882, by Harper & Brothers.

The Liberal Prime Minister William Ewart Gladstone, 'England's Great Commoner', who refused to authorise a relief force for General Gordon.

Aa reproduction of Alphone de Neuville's *British Foot Guards at the Battle of Tel-el-Kebir* (1882)

hammering of Italy's attempted colonial conquest of their country in the same year made some British statesmen believe that a re-conquest of the area was the right thing to do – after all, Ethiopia's victory over the Italians might inspire other African peoples to rise up and try to overthrow their European conquerors. Under the command of Herbert Kitchener, who is best known as the face of the First World War propaganda posters, an Anglo-Egyptian expeditionary force set out in 1896 to bring order back to the region. By 1899, after some bloody and not very glorious victories, Sudan was brought back under Anglo-Egyptian control.

For much of the nineteenth century, British popular patriotism was focused only on Britain, often only on England. This changed in the late-Victorian period when writers attempted to inspire in readers a fervent sense of loyalty to the nation, to the Queen, *and* to the empire. A steadfast belief in the greatness of Britain and its empire would, it was hoped, instil soldiers with courage even in the face of death, which was the noblest sacrifice one could make in the service of their country:

A certain fate awaits them all – they know it, but they will die as brave men should; but while they live, their hearts, and their hands, belong to the country which they love and the Queen whom they serve. One man, nobly inspired, starts the noble and familiar strain, and in a moment the tune is caught up, and they meet their death singing GOD SAVE THE QUEEN.[32]

Yet there were some heroes, or rather anti-heroes, who were not so noble and not devoted to the empire. Some of them fought against colonial authority and their stories were just as popular as those told of Gordon and Clive. Let us now meet the rogues, pirates, and criminals who carried on their crimes on the Seven Seas and in parts of the colonies where colonial authorities rarely ventured. They were the bad boys of the empire.

Chapter 6

The Bad Boys of the Empire

Before the reader proceeds further, I will warn him that he will not find my robbers such romantic, generous characters as those that occasionally figure in the fields of fiction.

Charles Macfarlane, *Lives and Exploits of the Most Celebrated Robbers and Banditti of all Countries* (1833)

A generation has gone by since [Ned Kelly and his men] baffled the police forces of Victoria and New South Wales; the glamour of their lawless lives shows little sign of waning. For they proved they had the stuff from which great heroes can be moulded. And they perished fighting to the last.

Famous Crimes (1900)

In the early modern period, the empire was primarily a means to extend British commercial interests overseas. Later in the nineteenth century, imperialists largely justified the empire's existence by promoting the so-called 'civilising mission', or the 'White Man's Burden'.[1] Yet the empire also provided a brilliant hiding place for pirates – forerunners of today's transnational criminals – who owed loyalty to no state or nation and smuggled goods into countries illegally. Piracy flourished during the golden age of sail in the eighteenth century. While real-life pirates may have been fearsome to encounter, in popular literature people loved them.

One of the first commercially successful works which recounted the lives of rogues who ravaged their way through the empire was Charles Johnson's *General History of the Robberies and Murders of the Most Notorious Pyrates* (1724). Nothing is known of Johnson's life, who styled himself as 'Captain' in his literary works. Scholars have not altogether unreasonably argued that Johnson was Daniel Defoe writing under pseudonym. Whoever Johnson was, although his *Pyrates* is styled as a 'history', it is not a factual history of the type that people would read today. Johnson invented quite a few of the 'facts' in his narrative, often made up the details of certain pirates' early lives and exaggerated their exploits, although his preface does reveal a competent knowledge of sea laws during the early eighteenth century.[2] Johnson's cavalier use of facts in his writings was not unique in this period, when many authors presented their narratives as histories when they were largely fictional. The full title of Defoe's *Moll Flanders* (1722) gives the impression that it is a thoroughly researched 'true account' of a woman who travelled, not by choice, to a distant parts of the empire:

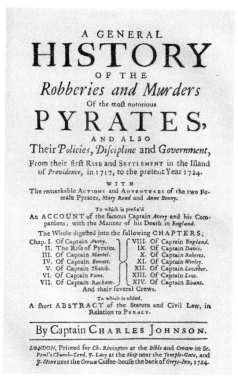

The title page of Charles Johnson's *General History of the Robberies and Murders of the Most Notorious Pyrates* (1724).

The Fortunes and Misfortunes of the Famous Moll Flanders; Who was born in Newgate, and during a life of continu'd Variety for Threescore Years, besides her Childhood, was Twelve Years a Whore, five times a Wife (whereof once to her brother) Twelve Years a Thief, Eight Years a Transported Felon in Virginia, at last grew Rich, liv'd Honest and died a Penitent. Written from her own Memorandums.

(Writers in the eighteenth century were fond of very long titles, which served a function similar to that of the 'blurb' on a modern book today, giving readers a taste of what they could expect if they purchased a copy).

Johnson's *Pyrates* were part of a flourishing genre of literature known as criminal biography. Public interest in crime reached an all-time high because people assumed, largely thanks to journalists, that the country

Ann Bonny *and* Mary Read *convicted of Piracy Nov.ʳ 28ᵗʰ 1720 at a Court of Vice Admiralty held at* S.ᵗ Jago de la Vega *in y̔ Island of Jamaica.*

Two notorious female pirates who dressed in men's clothes and took to a life of piracy on the Seven Seas.

was in the midst of a crime epidemic.[3] Then, as now, journalists were prone to exaggerating the problem to sell papers.[4] The result of this moral panic was the proliferation of books similar to Johnson's and monthly magazines such as *The Ordinary of Newgate's Account*. Criminal biographers' professed purpose in writing such works was first and foremost, as Johnson said in his preface, to provide moral instruction to readers, that they might not end up at the gallows like the pirates and rogues in his books did.[5] However, we can take their didacticism with a pinch of salt. They should be viewed like today's tabloid newspapers: their writers had no difficulty denouncing sex and violence but took great pleasure in showing it. Johnson's retelling of the life of notorious pirate Mary Read, who lived most of her life disguised as a man, is one example where he did not shy away from titillating readers. This is the scene described when one male pirate discovers Read's true identity:

She suffered the discovery to be made, by carelessly showing her breasts, which were very white. The young fellow, who was made of flesh and blood, had his curiosity and desire so raised by this sight that he never ceased importuning her till she confessed what she was. Now begins the scene of love. As he had a liking and esteem for her under her supposed character, it was now turned into fondness and desire. Her passion was no less violent than his, and perhaps she expressed it by one of the most generous actions that ever love inspired.[6]

Mary Read's story was the inspiration for nineteenth-century broadside ballads such as *The Female Smuggler*. The woman in question turns to a life of smuggling and piracy because she has to financially support her poor old father. However, the ballad has a happier ending than that which would befall Read, who died of a fever in a Jamaican gaol while pregnant; the ballad sees the female smuggler fall in love with a naval captain, who saves her from being hanged, and eventually marries her:

> Their commodore against her appeared,
> And for her life she did greatly fear.
> When he did find to his great surprise
> 'Twas a female smuggler,
> 'Twas a female smuggler had fought him in disguise.
>
> He to the judge and the jury said,
> "I cannot prosecute this maid,
> Pardon for her on my knees I crave,
> For this female smuggler,
> For this female smuggler so valiant and so brave."
>
> Then this commodore to her father went,
> To gain her hand he asked his consent.
> His consent he gained, so the commodore
> And the female smuggler,
> And the female smuggler are one for evermore.[7]

Johnson's attitude towards the pirates he wrote about vacillated between admiration and condemnation. Men such as the buccaneer Philip Roche were 'savage' people.[8] Yet Johnson admired the bravery of these men and women who took to the seas, and the exotic settings excited readers. Johnson even argued that a certain amount of piracy in the empire was healthy for society because it meant that rogues, who might be unemployed in peacetime, could be unruly and break the law to their hearts' content away from Britain, out of sight and out of mind.[9]

Pirates remained popular with audiences well into the nineteenth century when Johnson's book was reprinted in a number of cheap editions. Stories of these brave but brutal souls were retold in novels, penny novels, and ballads. The infamous William Kidd (1654–1701) was one such pirate who enjoyed a literary 'afterlife'. Kidd was born in Dundee, Scotland, and emigrated to New York in his later teenage years where he became a respected member of colonial society. During King William's War – part of the larger Nine Years' War (1688–97) – the colonial government employed Kidd as a privateer. He was never a very successful privateer, and after the war, being short of money, he turned to piracy. As a pirate, Kidd was a thug, murdering his gunner, William Moore, after a petty dispute. He was eventually captured and sent to England for trial, found guilty of five counts of piracy and murder, and hanged at Execution Dock.

Almost from the day he died, people sang songs about him. The popular *Ballad of William Kidd*, reprinted throughout the Georgian and Victorian periods, depicted him as a brave and heroic figure, but one whom, in view of his murder and sinful life, was justly punished for his crimes (we noted previously that many ballads were cheaply printed, and in the particular version quoted below the publishers have not even bothered to get their basic facts regarding Kidd's name correct – they have called him Robert. Folk song scholars and enthusiasts spend much time ballads' textual variations but many times the variants are probably due to the laziness of printers' apprentices):

You captains bold and brave hear our cries, hear our cries,
You captains bold and brave hear our cries,
You captains bold and brave, tho' you seem uncontroll'd
Don't for the sake of gold lose your souls, lose your souls,
Don't for the sake of gold lose your souls.

My name was Robert Kidd when I sail'd, when I sail'd,
My name was Robert Kidd when I sail'd,
My name was Robert Kidd when I sail'd, God's law I did forbid,
And so wickedly I did when I sailed when I sailed.

My parents taught me well, when I sail'd when I sail'd,
My parents taught me well, when I sailed,
My parents taught me well, to shun the gates of hell,
But against them I rebell'd when I sail'd.

I curs'd my father when I sail'd when I sailed,
I curs'd my father when I sail'd.
I curs'd my father dear and her that did me bear,
And so wickedly did swear when I sail'd.

I made a solemn vow when I sail'd when I sailed,
I made a solemn vow when I sail'd
I made a solemn vow to God I would not bow,
Nor myself one prayer allow when I sail'd.[10]

Before the emergence of academic criminology in the second half of
the nineteenth century, law-makers, journalists, and the public-at-large
assumed that people committed crime when they indulged their sinful
inclinations. The effects of small youthful sins such as being rebellious
towards one's parents, not reading the Bible or saying one's prayers meant
that, in later life, criminals would be inclined to commit larger offences
against other forms of authority such as the state. It was a slippery slope
because once one had started on this downward spiral, no matter if they
tried to get back on to the straight and narrow, it was all too easy to slip
off again, hence Kidd's own words in the ballad:

My repentance lasted not, as I sailed as I sail'd,
Damnation's my just lot, as I sailed.
My repentance lasted not, as I sailed as I sail'd,
Damnation's my just lot, as I sailed.[11]

Occasionally there were subtle hints of patriotism in pirate stories and ballads. *The Pirate of the Isles*, which dates from c. 1830 and was reprinted until the death of the broadside trade c. 1860, celebrates giving the French and Spanish a bloody nose.[12] Pirates were also depicted as womanizers and several songs such as *The Pirate's Bride* tell of brief, on-shore romances with gallant 'sea kings'.[13] Weekly serials, such as Edward Lloyd's *The History and Lives of the Most Notorious Pirates of All Nations* published in 1835, downplayed their worst crimes and framed their stories more as innocent and relatively bloodless tales of adventure. Every issue of Lloyd's serial featured a woodcut on its front page depicting the most exciting part of the story each week. Other cheap publishers recognised that Lloyd was onto a winning formula and began publishing imitations of his *Pirates* magazine. One such magazine, *Tales of the Pirates, or Lives of Smugglers and Buccaneers* appeared in 1840 and enjoyed a good run of issues which was then revived in 1847 for a further thirty-one issues. Writers such as Thomas Peckett Prest, author of the original Sweeney Todd novel, wove supernatural elements into their tales of piracy to capitalise on the prevailing public appetite for all things gothic and beastly. Prest's *The Wood Devil; or, The Vampire Pirate of the Deep Dell*, published in *The Penny Play-Book; or, Library of Dramatic Romance*, gave readers a blood-sucking vampire who was the terror of the Seven Seas!

These pirate-themed penny bloods influenced the more youth-oriented penny dreadfuls in the latter part of the Victorian era. These penny dreadful pirates were often given highly improbable backstories in which, although set in the eighteenth century, they are often seen to attend what looks suspiciously like a late-Victorian public school, much like the Rebel Jack who appeared in *The Boys' Comic Journal*. Jack was hardly a dutiful public school youngster and regularly misbehaved in class:

"I will call on your father tonight and he shall learn your true character," [said the schoolmaster].
"Tell it me now before all my schoolmates here."
"You are a ne'er-do-well, and, unless you alter your ways, you will die by the hands of the common hangman!"
Rebel Jack laughed scornfully.[14]

Captain Long John Silver from Robert Louis Stevenson's *Treasure Island* (1883), a character who influenced many successive portrayals of pirates in twentieth-century popular culture.

Nevertheless, these fictional pirates were always fair and dealt with both their comrades and their enemies in a civil manner. In the anonymously written *Kit the Pirate; or, Life on the Ocean* (1865), for example, one of the first rules of a pirate's life is to extend the principle of fair play to all other pirates.[15]

Even mainstream Victorian novelists could not avoid the allure of pirates. Robert Louis Stevenson's *Treasure Island* (1883) introduced readers to one of the most famous fictional pirates of the age: Long John Silver. Stevenson began his literary career as a travel writer but, as he acknowledged himself, there was little money in this and the public much preferred a fun tale of adventure, which he was only too ready to provide.[16] He prefaced *Treasure Island* by invoking the names of adventure novelists from the earlier part of the century:

> If sailor tales to sailor tunes,
> Storm and adventure, heat and cold,
> If schooners, islands, and maroons,
> And buccaneers, and buried gold,
> And all the old romance, retold
> Exactly in the ancient way,
> Can please, as me they pleased of old,
> The wiser youngsters of today.
>
> – So be it, and fall on! If not,
> If studious youth no longer crave,
> His ancient appetites forgot,
> Kingston, or Ballantyne the brave,
> Or Cooper of the wood and wave:
> So be it, also! And may I
> And all my pirates share the grave
> Where these and their creations lie![17]

Some of the pirates in the novel are clearly alcoholics, having lived their lives drinking rum daily. Although Stevenson's novel was a children's book, readers were given the sight of an ageing pirate going through alcohol withdrawal which is a subtle continuity of the didacticism inherent in earlier pirate tales: these men might live an exciting life but their lifestyle would catch up with them.

The novel, set during the eighteenth century, tells the story of young Jim who finds a treasure map in an old pirate's belongings. Jim teams up with Squire Trelawney and Dr Livesey and the three of them charter a boat and sail off in search of the lost treasure. The person whom they employ to be the ship's cook is a Bristol pub landlord who turns out to be Long John Silver. The crew of the ship, led by Silver, decide that they will mutiny once they reach their destination and take the treasure for themselves. Having overheard the crew's plans to mutiny, when they reach the island, Jim rushes ashore and disappears into the jungle with the map. Stevenson gave brilliant descriptions of Silver's appearance, and it is to Stevenson we in modern times owe our stereotype of the pirate:

> His left leg was cut off close by the hip, and under the left shoulder he carried a crutch, which he managed with wonderful dexterity, hopping about upon it like a bird. He was very tall and strong, with a face as big as a ham – plain and pale, but intelligent and smiling.[18]

Silver's pet parrot perches on his shoulder, and the image of a pirate with a parrot or other animal on his shoulder has become a recurring motif. At first glance, Silver appears to be only interested in loot and plunder. But Stevenson had created a more nuanced character: one of the reasons why he wants to steal all of the treasure is because he wants to leave his pirating life behind and become 'a gentleman':

> 'Now, the most goes for rum and a good fling, and to sea again in their shirts. But that's not the course I lay. I puts it all away, some here, some there, and none too much anywheres, by reason of suspicion. I'm fifty, mark you; once back from this cruise, I set up gentleman in earnest.[19]

Stevenson was criticising Victorian ideas of gentlemanliness and respectability. Long John Silver is both a hero and antihero. He can venture into foreign climes in spite of his disability, which challenges the idea in contemporary fiction that a man had to be fit, healthy, and 'lord of creation' to survive out in the big wide world. This was at a time when disabled people were more often than not depicted in popular culture as beggars and vagrants, potentially criminal, economically worthless, members of 'the deserving poor' who should be cared for in workhouses, or even participants in 'freak' shows, displayed as a spectacle to satisfy the titilation and morbid fascination of contemporary audiences.

All the men in *Treasure Island* who embark on the voyage to find the treasure have the same motivation: to make money and improve their lot in life. It is what Silver hopes to do and it is what the respectable Jim, Dr Livesey, and Squire Trelawney desire to do as well. Each of them is willing to fight to the death for this treasure and even 'invade' a remote island to get what they want. While the novels of Henty portrayed the schoolboy who ventured out to far-flung regions as altruistic, selfless, noble, and patriotic, Stevenson gave us the alternative view of colonialists' motivations: greed. There was little difference between a pirate and a colonist.

Stevenson's novel also contains a criticism of 'the flight from domesticity' which had seemingly beguiled so many men to venture abroad in the pursuit of wealth to the neglect of families. Young Jim, who is from a poor family, leaves his mother at the beginning of his adventure. At several points in the novel he faces great danger to his life yet he seems unconcerned at the fact that, if anything were to happen to him, it would leave his mother alone and penniless in the world. Long John Silver is a family man, married to an African woman whom he has had to likewise abandon in favour of 'seeking his fortune'. Indeed at this time some journalists blamed the high incidence of spinsterhood in Britain on the fact that too many young men were wandering off to the colonies instead of staying at home and raising a family.[20] Stevenson was not the only one who took aim at the idea of men going off to the colonies without a second thought for their families. Frances Hodgson Burnett wrote two works dealing with this problem: *A Little Princess* (1905) and *The Secret Garden* (1911). In each of these novels, and in penny novels such as *The Sea Gull* (1879), the parents of the young girls, around whom the stories revolve, die as a result of imperial service and the children are cast into unpleasant circumstances.[21] Some of these sentiments, of course, were both a return to and an extension of the opinion expressed by Walter Scott in 1819, that men should refrain from going abroad at times when the nation needed them back home. Seemingly childish novels such as *Treasure Island* and those by Hodgson Burnett therefore subverted the 'manly' imperial ideals found in the works of Henty and others.

It is intimated at the end of Stevenson's novel that, having come away with some treasure money, Silver does indeed set himself up as a gentleman. However, not all of the colonial criminals featured in Victorian literature were lovable rogues like Long John Silver. After the publication of Johnson's *Highwaymen*, a number of publications bearing the title of *The Newgate Calendar*, named after the notorious London gaol, appeared after c. 1770. Like Johnson's earlier works, these were compilations of short biographies of pirates, rogues, and highwaymen of every description. The wickedness of many criminals in these books was often exaggerated, for most were guilty of only minor crimes. However, it is to

Charles Kinnaister (a.k.a. Kilmeister) and his accomplices massacring the aborigines.

a story about a set of brutes, or 'monsters in human shape', from New South Wales which we now turn. Their stories appeared in a two-volume work entitled *The Chronicles of Crime; or, The New Newgate Calendar* (1841), edited by Camden Pelham, which aimed to be a more serious and scholarly version of the *Newgate Calendars* which had gone before.[22]

The history of British imperialism is often conceived of as a period in which colonisers committed atrocities against the indigenous population without any consequences. That the British were responsible for some ghastly humanitarian crimes during their imperial heyday is certainly true, but the colonisers were not *completely* free to treat the indigenous people of the empire as they pleased. This was especially the case with men who had been transported. Pelham did not shy away from laying bare the atrocities committed by some of the reprobates sent to the penal colonies, nor did he refrain from denouncing racism. Pelham records the execution of Charles Kinnaister (named Kilmeister in some accounts) and his men in 1838 for the murder of Australian aborigines. Kinnaister and several accomplices had been transported to New South Wales in 1837 for petty crimes. While transportation was designed to be a punishment, one of the ideas behind it was that some of the felons transported could serve as labourers for the local citizens and help to develop the colony. Kinnaister and his men were assigned to work as shepherds for a family of landowners. One day the felons rode beyond their masters' lands and encountered a group of aborigines. Because they were a set of nasty thugs, Kinnaister and his crew

> tied them together with a rope, with the exception of one woman. This was done without a word being uttered, and with a cool and bloody determination. When all were thus secured, one end of the rope was tied around the body of the foremost of the murderers, who, having mounted his horse, led the way, dragging the terrified group after him, while his infamous companions guarded them on all sides.[23]

The victims were dragged some distance after which they were butchered with knives and swords, 'till all lay a lifeless mass, in death clinging to each other in the throes of natural affection'.[24] The savage murderers attempted to conceal their crimes as best they could by setting light to the bodies and leaving them to burn. But the fire was not good enough to totally eliminate the foul deeds; it died out leaving several fragments of bones while one corpse was left almost completely whole.

A professional police force in Britain had only been recently established in 1829, and one would not be established in New South Wales until 1862. When Kinnaister and his fellow thugs were active, many Europeans still believed that God directly intervened in the detection and punishment of murderers – a belief which stretched as far back as the early modern period – and we find Pelham expressing the same sentiments. Despite the men's attempts to conceal their foul deeds,

> The vengeance of providence was not to be thus thwarted; and although for a time these miscreants imagined they had effectually disguised their horrible work, circumstances led to their detection and apprehension.[25]

THE NEW
NEWGATE CALENDAR,
CONTAINING THE
REMARKABLE LIVES AND TRIALS OF NOTORIOUS CRIMINALS, PAST AND PRESENT.

No. 3.—Vol. I.]   SATURDAY, NOVEMBER 7, 1863.   [One Penny.

THE DISCOVERY.—GILBERT LANGLEY DEFENDS HIMSELF.

BEAU LANGLEY, SCHOLAR AND LIBERTINE.

CHAPTER I. (*Continued.*)

The town gates were closed, and we were surrounded by soldiers, delighted in having a chance to be revenged upon us for refusing to treat their comrade to some wine.

No. 3.—Vol. I.

The odds were decidedly against us, but I managed to trip up the heels of the officer who had collared me, and was about to floor another, when two friars from the convent arrived and interfered, saying that it was illegal to take us before a civil magistrate, the superior of our own college being accountable for our conduct. When taken before the Prior he severely censured us, but managed to hush the matter up with the town authorities.

Beau Langley whose adventures, which took him to far off lands, were chronicled in the penny dreadful version of *The New Newgate Calendar* in the 1860s.

Vultures were seen circling the place where the outrage had been committed. A group of stockmen went to investigate and found the half-burnt carcasses. Kinnaister and his accomplices were immediately suspected, owing to their past conduct, and upon examination the men admitted everything they had done. One detail which Pelham omitted was the fact that one of the gang, named George Anderson, who was in a relationship with a young Aboriginal woman called Ipeta, refused to take part in the massacre and his eyewitness testimony was crucial in ensuring they were brought to justice. The 'whole' body that was left unburnt by the men was that of a man named 'Daddy', and so it was for his murder that the men were indicted.

Despite Kinnaister and his men's admission of guilt, as well as the strong circumstantial evidence against them, an association was formed by some of the wealthier free colonists to secure the murderers an acquittal. The best legal counsel was hired, and the defence lawyers argued that the murders were necessary because 'they had been formed with the ostensible project of preserving the property of the settlers from the incursions of the natives'.[26] This defence convinced the jury and the men were found not guilty. It was a case of blatant racial prejudice. Camden Pelham expressed his regret and shame that racial prejudices contributed to the acquittal; these 'diabolical murderers' did not deserve to be called Englishmen.[27] The prosecution did not rest however: two months later the men were arraigned again, and this time they were justly found guilty by the jury. The vile criminals were then hanged on 15 December 1838. History books may often be written by people from 'victor' nations but they do not always present the victors in a positive light.

One popular penny dreadful was the serialised edition of *The New Newgate Calendar*, which printed short fiction based upon the crimes related in earlier *Newgate Calendars*. Gilbert Langley, *alias* Beau Langley, was one of the criminals featured in this magazine's columns. Born in Derbyshire c. 1720, the real Langley was a public school boy, having attended Charterhouse where he diligently applied himself to his studies, becoming 'a good classical scholar'.[28] He was also a brilliant 'sportsman of the turf', according to other accounts.[29] Had Langley's life followed a different path, he might well have been taken up as the heroic protagonist of a late-Victorian novel – but this was not to be. In *The New Newgate Calendar* he is an idler who, unable to secure proper employment, makes his money at the gaming table, then frittering it away while fraternising with prostitutes and other low-lives of the criminal underworld in public houses. Langley's wife grows tired of his antics – and who can blame her – so she absconds with a sailor, never to see Langley again. As a result of his gambling debts, and being pursued by creditors, Langley hastily leaves for the West Indies.[30] The colonies are a convenient place to escape to for rogues like himself who find themselves on the wrong end of the law. He then finds himself on the wrong side of the law in Jamaica, and boards a ship for England, but when he gets there he is arrested for his debt and placed in a debtors' prison. But a man used to a life of drinking, gambling and sleeping around finds prison life not to his liking. He escapes from gaol and then boards a ship bound, once again, for Jamaica. Every possible chance is given to him to turn his life around and seek honest employment, but, being almost addicted to thievery, he screws it up spectacularly:

> While [in Jamaica], I was employed by a Colonel Hill to educate his children. I stayed in the Colonel's family six months, and then, helping myself to some loose cash and a few stray articles of jewellery, I got aboard ship and returned to England.[31]

Back in England, he turns to highway robbery to support himself. He is not a very good highwayman however, and is caught within three weeks. Luckily for Langley, he is not hanged at Tyburn but transported to Virginia for seven years, after which he is given a plot of land and eventually manages to build a flourishing tobacco business, having learnt the error of his ways. In true picaresque style, Langley repents of his former misdeeds and resolves to be a good Christian and productive member of society.

As we have seen, in early-to-mid-Victorian literature, it was often the case that writers represented the colonies as places where the worst type of people went. Transportation to the West Indies and Americas ended in the late eighteenth century when the government opted to send its convicts to Australia. Transportation to New South Wales finally ended in 1868 as the Australian government understandably objected to the arrivals of convicts. Back home in the British penal system, prison reformers had largely succeeded in convincing the government of the need to both punish and rehabilitate offenders through long-term institutional management; offenders became society's responsibility, and between the 1840s and 1860s, several large prisons were erected throughout the United Kingdom. As the incidence of transportation declined and ceased to be a fact of life, so its relevance for contemporary novelists' plots waned.

JACK HARKAWAY.

Stories of 'Jack the lads' in penny dreadfuls were serious rivals for popularity to any of the rather wet heroes of *The Boy's Own Paper*. Some dreadfuls told stories of rogue boy smugglers living in English coastal towns.[32] The protagonists were often from more humble circumstances than the public school boys of Henty's stories but were often just as fit and competitive as their counterparts in the five shilling works. One such boy was young Henry who appeared in *The Captain of Blackrock Castle* (1879):

Jack Harkaway: one of the most popular penny dreadful heroes, whose many adventures, told in countless works, entertained many a young lad in late-Victorian England.

> Henry quickly acquired a remarkable proficiency, considering his age, in the various branches of learning, but also a complete mastery of all the exercises in physical agility, strength, and endurance. Endowed by nature with a most robust constitution, a tall and well-knit frame, and no small share of good looks, he grew under this judicious culture into a fine, noble-looking lad; and, at fourteen years of age, was at the head of all his schoolfellows both in the class and in the field.[33]

The Boy's Halfpenny Journal quickly floundered in the cut-throat world of penny publishing: it was hard to compete with the most famous penny dreadful hero at this time: young Mr Jack Harkaway, a character who first appeared in *The Boys of England*. There are tales of newsagents fighting with each other to secure the latest instalment of his adventures because he was such a hit with all readers, young and old – the Harry Potter of his generation. Harkaway, who remains one of the most entertaining Victorian characters ever created, offered a refreshing change from the contemporary public school hero. He came from a family of moderate means, for although he was of aristocratic birth – much like many a Victorian protagonist – he had been born out of wedlock and, to keep the scandal quiet, his parents had placed him in the care of a lower-middle-class family.

In the first instalment, *Jack Harkaway's Schooldays* (c. 1880), there is very little comment upon his physique or athleticism in general.[34] The author of the *Jack Harkaway* series, Bracebridge Hemyng, however did focus upon Jack's general attitude saying that 'he was often disobedient, nearly always mischievous, and at times disrespectful'.[35] Where Jack's physical abilities do end up being of use to him at school, it is usually in fights with people he sees as bullies; he is ever ready to defend the weak against the strong. In this respect his character bears some similarity to the chivalrous heroes of hardback novels. Harkaway was as patriotic as any of Henty's heroes and he fights for Queen and country in *Jack Harkaway in the Transvaal: or, Fighting for the Flag* (1900), set during the Boer War. When Jack captures a lone Boer, he does not pass up a chance to humiliate his captive by making him sing *Rule Britannia* and *God Save the Queen*:

> "Don't get up. Keep on your knees; I like to see you that way. Now, follow me, pay attention: say 'Rule Britannia' and 'God Save the Queen.'"
>
> "What!" cried [the Boer] ... "Here you are. 'Rule Britannia' and 'God Save Your Queen.' Ugh! There is a lump in my throat. You make me sick. That Queen sticks. She will choke me. I say it, but don't mean it."
>
> "Now, sing it," continued Jack, putting the rifle a few inches nearer to his head. "I set you a go. Don't mumble, but raise it. Give us a chest note. 'Send her Victorious, happy and glorious, long to reign over us, God Save the Queen.'"

With the utmost reluctance, and making as many grimaces as a monkey with the spasms, the Boer followed Jack, and then rolled on the floor, burying his face in his hands.

"Hurrah! That's your sort. Bravo our side. 'Rule Britannia, Britannia rules the waves, and the Transvaal Boers shall never make us slaves.'"[36]

Harkaway was a rascal, but he loved his queen. Yet there are other penny dreadful heroes who were not patriotic in the slightest, a case in point being one of the most famous bad boys of the British Empire: the outlaw Ned Kelly (1854–80). His fame, or infamy, spread the world over. He wore a suit of iron-plated armour and his helmet had only a small slit along the eyes so he could see out, and he must have presented a fearsome sight to the lonely traveller. Kelly's father was a former transportee who died when he was 12 years old, leaving him as the man of the house, charged with protecting his mother as well as his siblings. By all accounts, Kelly himself was something of a tearaway and associated with several men of dubious reputation in various underworld taverns, and his profligate youth was always emphasised in popular literature. But he is a brave outlaw in who laughs in the face of danger. Some of his portrayals in cheap literature did bear some similarity with the public school ethos, for he is a fit and energetic man and the members of his outlaw band are not wanting in strength and endurance. These skills serve them well living in the Australian outback and evading the law. In his own criminal way he is at least chivalrous. *Famous Crimes* devoted several issues to the Kelly's life story and the reader was told that whenever Kelly robbed anybody, he was at least polite about it: 'as long as there was fair play, Ned had chivalrously refrained from using his pistol'.[37] The idea that highwaymen refrained as much as possible from using unnecessary violence has a long history and often the mere threat of a pistol was supposed to suffice.[38] Yet many outlaws' purported chivalrous conduct was largely a fiction which masked a more unpleasant truth: the so-called 'Knights of the Road' were rather brutal fellows. But authors and readers alike believed in the contrived idea of the chivalrous outlaw because it palliated their fears: the colonies were often imagined as dangerous places; if it was not the indigenous peoples of the empire which posed a threat, there were cut-throat robbers and outlaws ever ready to attack the unwary traveller. People *needed* to believe in the myth of a good criminal in the colonies, even if those beliefs were based on a fiction, because the truth was ultimately too worrisome.

A long-running serial, *Ned Kelly: The Iron-Clad Australian Bushranger*, was published in 1881 – just one year after the real Kelly died, which illustrates just how quickly his fame spread.[39] Readers first meet Kelly in a tavern of ill repute, where the inebriated patrons rowdily sing songs celebrating the life of Australian

Ned Kelly in his suit of armour, from a photograph in Francis A. Hare's *The Last of the Bushrangers* (1895).

and English outlaws. Despite the company he keeps however, Kelly is not an irredeemably bad person; the reason he is an outlaw is that he was falsely accused of a crime by a corrupt police officer and proclaimed as an outlaw.[40] This is how many noble robbers' criminal careers are said to begin, as Eric Hobsbawm states: 'the noble robber begins his career of outlawry not by crime, but as the victim of injustice, or through being persecuted by the authorities'.

Kelly's first loyalty is to his daughter and his mission in life is to protect her; this harks back to earlier conceptions of manliness which celebrated domesticity and held that fathers' and husbands' first duty was to their family. Furthermore, in popular tales of bandits, the outlaw, while robbing from the rich, is usually depicted as someone loyal to the monarch. As Eric Hobsbawm notes, the noble robber 'is [usually] not the enemy of the king or emperor, who is the fount of justice, but only of the local gentry, clergy, or other oppressors'. But there is no comparable love for Queen Victoria in the Ned Kelly story. While Kelly does steal from the rich and give to the poor in this novel, his lack of loyalty to the monarch is one way in which this particular portrayal of Kelly separates him from other noble bandits.

Kelly certainly does not hold back from criticising the ruling elite in the mother country. The success of the novel, which ran to over thirty-eight issues, meant that the author, who was probably paid by the line, inserted unlikely subplots into the narrative. This is why we see Kelly travel to London. When he sees that many poorer children are left to fend for themselves on the streets, he remarks to his associate,

> There is plenty of work for Christian men here, without going abroad to convert woolly-headed, naked heathens. The money that is spent on African missions might save many poor English children from a fate worse than death.[41]

Clearly, Britain's ruling class was not loyal and protective of its own citizens; highly critical of the world's Mrs Jellybys, there was little justification for Kelly to be patriotic when he saw how Britain's poorer citizens were treated.

The reprobates chronicled here offered readers a refreshing alternative to popular portrayals of public school heroes or biographical narratives of imperialists. Younger readers in the late nineteenth century were just as likely to have encountered the empire as much in crime writing and tales of pirates, highwaymen, and outlaws, as they were in the works of Henty and Rider Haggard. More stinging criticisms of imperialism and the empire's soldiers were to be found, however, in the nineteenth-century radical press.

Chapter 7

'Desperadoes and Homicidal Madmen'

Ever since the time Robert Clive forsook the pen for the sword, and exchanged the ledger for the war chest, our career in India has been one of ceaseless aggression, plunder, and oppression. No sooner has once province or kingdom fallen under our rule than another is found to be in that condition which affords a pretext for our seizing it also.

The Northern Star (1851)

"The rivalry among the nations for their share of the world market" (to quote the words of our manifesto) must now, one would think, have discovered itself to even the casual newspaper reader as the only meaning the terms "diplomacy" and "foreign policy" any longer possess. The jealousy between the courts of Europe, once the sole and until recently the main cause of national enmity and war, has in our day been superseded by the jealousy between the great capitalists of its various nationalities. The flunkey-patriot, zealous of his country's honour, dances as readily to-day to the pipe of capitalist greed as he did before to that of royal intrigue.

E. Belfort Bax, *Socialism and Imperialism* (1885)

With the exception of criminals, we have encountered fairly mainstream Victorian views of the empire and of the men who expanded it. They were imagined in Victorian popular literature as manly, chivalrous warriors defending Britain's empire and ever ready to make the ultimate sacrifice. Yet we saw how, even in the early seventeenth century when the British Empire was just beginning, the colonisation of the Americas made Beaumont and Fletcher uneasy. Criticisms of the empire continued to be made throughout the next century. Even though Defoe created Robinson Crusoe, the archetypal

The Duke of Wellington: the hero of the Napoleonic Wars who was loved by many but also reviled by radicals.

imperialist, he had also voiced brief concerns about empire spreading 'her tempting wings' in *Jure Divino* (1706). In the Georgian period, Thomas Paine's *Common Sense* (1776) convinced a number of citizens in the Thirteen Colonies to rebel against their British rulers, and the economist Adam Smith in *The Wealth of Nations* (1776) denounced the 'showy equipage of empire'. It was during the nineteenth century however, with the rise of the radical press, that ever-increasing numbers of journalists and novelists voiced their opposition to British imperialism.

The Duke of Wellington was a hero to later Victorian writers. Unlike his Napoleonic-era counterpart Nelson, who died in the hour of his victory, Wellington went into politics after the wars and became leader of the Tory Party. He then served as Prime Minister from 1828 until 1830 during which time his government passed the Catholic Emancipation Act. In spite of his heroic victories, he was widely reviled by journalists in the radical press. Much of the criticism Wellington faced was the result of his opposition to the Whigs' proposed Reform Act in the 1830s, which would have extended the franchise in the 1830s, which would have extended the franchise to middle-class householders.

When it was sent up to the second chamber for its first reading, Tory lords rejected it. To radicals, and even those in favour of moderate political reform, this was unforgiveable. Although the Reform Act was passed in 1832 under the Whigs, in the years leading up to the emergence of Chartism, radicals sought to present what they saw as the duke's true character:

> No, thou art only havoc's lord,
> Thy trust is solely in thy sword,
> Rest, and as Warrior be ador'd.
>
> As Statesman, all who know thee hate,
> Though nerv'd to guide the ranks of hate,
> Thou hast not brain to legislate.
>
> Thou has not, as Napoleon had,
> The soul to make a nation glad,
> Dost think thou hast? If so, how mad![1]

Those lines were written in 1835 by the radical poet, Charles Cole. He and many of his other like-minded fellows were writing at a time of intense political agitation which included a campaign for universal male suffrage and for the removal of the Corn Laws, which were tariffs on grain imports designed to keep the price of bread high and suit the pockets of the landowners, many of whom were politicians.

Working-class writers often expressed solidarity with the oppressed peoples of the empire who were likewise denied a say over who governed them, as well as those held in slavery. Their expressions of solidarity took many forms, such as newspaper articles and pamphlets highlighting their plight. In response to the Jamaican Slave Revolt in the latter part of 1831, one essay writer in Henry Hetherington's *Poor Man's Guardian*, in its 25 February 1832 issue, took aim at those British 'tyrants' abroad who enslaved black people:

> Our brethren of Jamaica have revolted, and taken into their own hands the abolition of that slavery which a *Christian* people has imposed, and a *Christian* government of Whig *liberals* has countenanced, while they have pretended to remedy it. May fortune prosper their emancipation! "Jamaica is lost to us," exclaim the few who have usurped possession of its soil, and constrained its natives to culture it for their own exclusive advantage. – Jamaica lost to them! What right had they ever to call it theirs? It was at most "stolen property," and their own laws decide that it still belongs to those from whom it was taken; it was *lost* to those who are now retaking it and we trust that they may prove themselves more worthy of its possession than their tyrants have been, nor degrade themselves to the same state of *"Christian Civilization."*

By calling the rebel slaves 'brethren', the writer was clearly speaking of black people on equal terms; the brotherhood of the oppressed peoples of the empire was being expressed. The writer's use of italics denotes an ironic emphasis upon the 'liberal' principles of the supposed Christian empire. Unfortunately for the rebel slaves, in a classic case of 'divide and rule', the Christian imperialists sought the help of Jamaican Maroons – an independent community descended from former rebel slaves – to help track down the rebels and supress the rebellion. Around 200 slaves were killed by British forces during the revolt, and the savage plantation owners executed over 300 more slaves after the rebels were rounded up.

PROCLAMATION.

BY His Excellency SIR FRANCIS BOND HEAD,
Baronet, Lieutenant Governor of Upper Canada, &c. &c.

To the Queen's Faithful Subjects in Upper Canada.

In a time of profound peace, while every one was quietly following his occupations, feeling secure under the protection of our Laws, a band of Rebels, instigated by a few malignant and disloyal men, has had the wickedness and audacity to assemble with Arms, and to attack and Murder the Queen's Subjects on the Highway—to Burn and Destroy their Property—to Rob the Public Mails—and to threaten to Plunder the Banks—and to Fire the City of Toronto.

Brave and Loyal People of Upper Canada. we have been long suffering from the acts and endeavours of concealed Traitors, but this is the first time that Rebellion has dared to shew itself openly in the land, in the absence of invasion by any Foreign Enemy.

Let every man do his duty now, and it will be the last time that we or our children shall see our lives or properties endangered, or the Authority of our Gracious Queen insulted by such treacherous and ungrateful men. MILITIA-MEN OF UPPER CANADA, no Country has ever shewn a finer example of Loyalty and Spirit than YOU have given upon this sudden call of Duty. Young and old of all ranks, are flocking to the Standard of their Country. What has taken place will enable our Queen to know Her Friends from Her Enemies—a public enemy is never so dangerous as a concealed Traitor—and now my friends let us complete well what is begun—let us not return to our rest till Treason and Traitors are revealed to the light of day, and rendered harmless throughout the land.

Be vigilant, patient and active—leave punishment to the Laws—our first object is, to arrest and secure all those who have been guilty of Rebellion. Murder and Robbery.—And to aid us in this, a Reward is hereby offered of

One Thousand Pounds,

to any one who will apprehend, and deliver up to Justice, WILLIAM LYON MACKENZE; and FIVE HUNDRED POUNDS to any one who will apprehend, and deliver up to Justice, DAVID GIBSON—or SAMUEL LOUNT—or JESSE LLOYD—or SILAS FLETCHER—and the same reward and a free pardon will be given to any of their accomplices who will render this public service, except he or they shall have committed, in his own person, the crime of Murder or Arson.

And all, but the Leaders above-named, who have been seduced to join in this unnatural Rebellion, are hereby called to return to their duty to their Sovereign—to obey the Laws—and to live henceforward as good and faithful Subjects—and they will find the Government of their Queen as indulgent as it is just

GOD SAVE THE QUEEN.

Thursday, 3 o'clock, P. M.
7th Dec. 1837.

☞ The Party of Rebels, under their Chief Leaders, is wholly dispersed, and flying before the Loyal Militia. The only thing that remains to be done, is to find them, and arrest them.

R. STANTON, Printer to the QUEEN'S Most Excellent Majesty.

(op. 261)

A royal proclamation to the people of British North America seeking the apprehension of Canadian rebel leaders in late 1837.

Solidarity with people overseas was also expressed through poetry, especially in Chartist newspapers. The Reform Act of 1832 fell far short of early radicals' aims for universal suffrage. So, in 1836, six working men and six MPs drew up the People's Charter, which in its final form had six aims: the extension of the vote to all adult working men (women did not enter the equation for most people at this point); the creation of equally-sized electoral districts; salaries for MPs; the abolition of the requirement that an MP be a property owner; the secret ballot; and annual elections. The campaign to secure this aim, known as Chartism, became the first mass working-class movement. Between 1839 and 1848, three petitions were sent to the government asking MPs to grant their demands, and each petition was rejected in spite of mass meetings held in support of the charter's aims.

Poetry was often given front page status in Chartist newspapers such as *The Northern Star*; it was through verse, as Michael Sanders argues, that the rank-and-file of Chartist members received both entertainment, education, and political instruction. Chartists criticised the British government for the unnecessary shedding of British soldiers' lives in putting down various colonial rebellions:

> The red blood of thy bravest sons
> Is shed in foreign wars
> To put down rising liberty
> And aid the tyrants' cause.
>
> Where'er we turn, where'er we gaze,
> Oppression still is plain,
> The Affghan and Canadian,
> Curse England's galling chain.[2]

The Chartists' principles were internationalist, the movement's sentiments stemming from religious convictions, and racism was anathema to its principles. A song in *The National Chartist Hymnbook*, for example, declared that black people were equal to whites (they were not perfect, of course, and there are some isolated instances of racism from some Chartist activists).[3] One of the movement's leading activists was a black man named William Cuffay (1788–1870), the son of freed slaves from St Kitts who had, after their manumission, relocated to London. Cuffay was a firebrand, a 'Physical Force' Chartist who believed that direct action would be necessary to secure the movement's objectives. He took a leading role in organising the procession to deliver the petition to the House of Commons in 1848. Frustrated with the movement's lack of success, Cuffay joined a secret revolutionary committee with a view to planning an armed uprising in London. The police, through its network of spies and paid informants, caught wind of this group's activities and arrested the ringleaders. Cuffay was convicted for 'levying war against the Queen' and was transported to Tasmania. During his trial,

William Lyon Mackenzie, one of the ringleaders of the rebellion in Canada in late 1837.

The Times ridiculed Cuffay and called him 'a nigger' while *Punch* called him a drunken 'man of colour'.[4] In spite of the mainstream media's racist remarks about his life and character however, Cuffay remained a popular figure in the Chartist movement whose leading writers, by and large, cared little for ridiculous ideas of white racial superiority.

The Chartists wholeheartedly supported those living in British North America, or Canada, in their struggle for political representation which ran in parallel with their own. These were the lines which one poet, under the telling pseudonym of George Washington, wrote in support of the Canadians in the 1840s:

> The rifle is heard, and the flag is unfurl'd –
> A land to be free is a boon to the world;
> Each Briton born true will respond to the strain,
> That curses the wretch who invented a chain!

The spirit of discord through Canada flies,
And the sire, and the son, and the aged arise;
They strive not for tongues, nor for creeds, but they call,
For justice and freedom, the birth-right of all.

'Tis a call on the bosom that's noble and good –
'Tis a call that speaks home – that is well understood –
'Tis a call on the dead – on the child that's unborn –
'Tis a wailing at midnight, impatient of morn!

Sons of brave forefathers! Gallant in fight!
Who curb'd the bold steed in its furniture bright;
Be it known in the land where your ensign shall wave,
That your blood is too hot for the veins of a slave!

Oh, Canada! Type of the rising and free,
The minstrel anew strings his lyre for thee;
In your forest primeval, no longer deferr'd,
Let the proud hymn of liberty loudly be heard.

The young voice of Truth for a while may be crush'd,
'Twill thunder ere long and disdain to be hush'd;
And dark the venal page that asperses your name,
Your own after records shall blot out with shame.

Your groans are unheeded – half-frenzied – forlorn –
You begg'd for your rights, you were treated with scorn;
But the gauntlet is thrown – and the signal unfurl'd –
"A LAND TO BE FREE IS A BOON TO THE WORLD!"[5]

The poet calls on all good men across the empire, regardless of 'tongue' – which since the eighteenth century was often synonymous with race – to rise up and cast off the shackles of figurative slavery perpetuated by a cold-hearted and uncaring elite in London, the same elites against whom the Chartists were campaigning for political representation. Another poem pseudonymously written under the name of 'An American Citizen'

After the Canadian Rebellion in 1838, the British Prime Minister Lord Melbourne saw fit to appoint the progressive Lord Durham to oversee an inquiry into the causes of the revolt and prevent it happening in future. His reforms were far-reaching; Canadians were given a limited form of self-government, and this paved the way for the formation of a federal Dominion of Canada. But the Chartist campaign for working-class suffrage in Britain was still ongoing. This Chartist-friendly illustration, published in London in 1840, sees Lord Durham as a potential ally in the Chartist cause at home, although Durham never would give his support to Chartism. Image supplied with thanks to the Wellcome Library.

likewise called on Canadians to rise up against their tyrannical British rulers:

> When the proud land of Britain would sternly maintain
> Over far distant lands her tyrannical reign;
> When she sends forth her slaves to destroy Freedom's sons,
> May each slave that she sends prove a mark for their guns; –
> Here's success unto freedom, her sons ever brave,
> May the Patriot's land prove the tomb of the slave.[6]

We do not know the nationality of these pseudonymous poets yet it is clear that they identified with the fledgling democracy that had broken away from Britain in 1783, rather than as a subject of the British Crown. The 'spirit of discord' seen flying through Canada in the first poem may seem surprising given that, in the annals of imperial histories, that country does not have a reputation for having been particularly unruly. After all, this was the colony whose lads proudly marched into war against the United States in 1812, and whose 'victory' in that war was celebrated in songs.[7] When one thinks of colonial rebellions, those which come to mind are usually the American Revolution and the Indian Mutiny of 1857, or the Mau Mau Rebellion in Africa (1952–60).

However, the spirit of discord did indeed fly through Canada between November 1837 and January 1838. During those months a large-scale rebellion broke out which pitted the French-Canadian Patriotes – the 'Patriot' reference in the song above may be a direct reference to this group – against the British Crown. Canada at this point was not a united dominion but essentially two colonies: Upper Canada and Lower Canada. There was no democratic government in Canada as the people were ruled by the British Governor and a team of unelected advisors. The governor exercised almost autocratic control over the population and was not obliged to pay any attention to their demands for political and taxation reform. When the colonists presented their grievances directly to the House of Commons, British parliamentarians sided with the governor. The Canadians were justifiably angry, and their grievances were given further stimulus due to a trade depression that affected farmers in the French-speaking regions. Tensions reached boiling point when a band of Patriotes took up arms and fought two brief skirmishes against British soldiers in November. This little revolt was quickly put down but, to make matters worse, British soldiers set fire to a number of French Canadian farms in retaliation. The Patriotes then mounted a further rebellion with the help of some volunteer soldiers from the United States, but they could not beat the well-organised and well-armed British forces. This was not the end of matter however. A rebellion in Upper Canada quickly followed, and its leader, William Lyon Mackenzie, took control of Navy Island near Niagara and even proclaimed the establishment of a Canadian Republic. But Mackenzie's republican experiment was short-lived, as Loyalist and British forces quickly put down this enthusiastic but largely disorganised rebellion.

When both disturbances were put down, the government back in London realised it had to listen to the Canadians. The Prime Minister, Lord Melbourne (1779–1848), sent the progressive Lord Durham (1792–1840) to investigate the situation there and make recommendations on how to deal with mounting discontent in the region. On Durham's recommendation, in 1840 both colonies were united into a single colony and the Canadians were given regional self-government as well as a supreme court. Later in 1867, the colony

George William MacArthur Reynolds, one of the Victorian era's most popular writers. He was a radical and anti-racist, who railed against social injustice both at home and abroad.

of Canada, along with the hitherto independent regions of Nova Scotia and New Brunswick, were united into a federal, self-governing dominion. Had the government not acted upon Durham's recommendations, it is quite conceivable that Canada would have violently split from the British Empire in the same way that their neighbours to the south had done in 1776.

For the editor of *Reynolds's Newspaper*, the 'vicious republican', Chartist, and democrat, G.W.M. Reynolds, the existence of empire symbolised everything that was wrong with British society as a whole. Reynolds was a man whose moral character cannot be faulted. In contrast to some of his contemporaries such as Dickens, Reynolds was not a racist, having once denounced 'the demoralizing idea that white men have a right to enslave the blacks'.[8] He believed that women were not intellectually inferior to men in any way,[9] and he even railed against the Victorian gender pay gap.[10] Every week, Reynolds would write an editorial for his paper in which he provided readers with his thoughts on the week's pressing issues and his remark that colonialism was one of 'the chief kind of inhuman punishments' ever meted out to people is fairly typical of his views on the subject.[11]

A home theatre script of George Dibdin's *Paul Jones* (1827), a fictionalised story of the British sea captain, John Paul Jones, who sides with the Thirteen Colonies during the American Revolution. His story was then adapted by Pierce Egan the Younger in a long-running weekly penny novel.

The popular penny fiction author Pierce Egan the Younger. According to *MacMillan's Magazine*, Egan's novels 'sold by the half million'.

Reynolds was clear that the nobility was to blame for the evils of colonialism. He hated the aristocracy with a passion, and saw the empire as just another means through which the aristocracy entrenched its power at the expense of both the British working classes and those living in the colonies. The misdeeds committed abroad by the predominantly aristocratic military class were simply another manifestation of the nobility's inherent avarice, which he viewed as an almost genetic trait which each successive generation of nobles had been infected with since the Norman Conquest of 1066. Antony Taylor cites an interesting quote from Reynolds which is illustrative of his attitude in this regard, in which Reynolds referred to 'the real criminals – the common tyrants of both the British and Hindoos – the royal, aristocratic, and commercial rulers and robbers of India.'[12] Reynolds was not a lone voice in drawing attention to British atrocities abroad: other writers referred to 'British Tyranny in India' and were highly critical of the manner in which British conquerors exercised power over the people of the subcontinent.[13] Essentially, the East India Company's reign had been of absolutely no benefit for Indian society as a whole.[14] Radicals' accusations about the East India Company's mismanagement of the subcontinent were of course proved right when the mutiny broke out. When radical journalists looked back on the history of British India, to them it was

A series of treacheries, appropriations, ignored treaties, fearful misgovernment, and exactions by which the British Government became absolute masters of India. There was no act of atrocity, or tyranny, of which the first Napoleon was guilty in Europe that was not paralleled by the British in India.[15]

A reproduction of Richard Caton Woodville's *The Relief of the Light Brigade*.

This was certainly an alternative view of the East India Company's history and its 'heroic' men such as Robert Clive that was to be found in the realm of popular fiction and history books. The agents of the 'Honourable Company', one newspaper was at pains to point out, rarely acted according to the rules of fair play.[16] When the news of new imperial acquisitions reached home, *Reynolds's Newspaper* deplored the fact that the ruling classes of England were 'never without some little or contemptible war' to wage against an oppressed people overseas.[17]

Reynolds, and his friend Pierce Egan the Younger, scoffed at the idea that people should be loyal to the monarchy and a corrupt government. The younger Egan was one of the most prolific authors of the Victorian era. His political beliefs bordered on the radical, and he was chairman of the Repeal Association in the 1850s which campaigned to repeal the Union with Ireland Act. Egan's *Paul Jones the Privateer* (1842) told the story of the eponymous sea captain who defected to the colonists' side during the American War of Independence. Jones's reason for betraying his country in the novel is because 'the mother country was a hotbed of injustice' and 'unjustly oppressed the colonies'.[18] Although Egan had little love for the political establishment, he respected the army. His novel *Clifton Grey* (1856), set during the Crimean War, was dedicated 'to the soldiers of the army of England in admiration of their unflinching bravery in the battle-field, and their noble fortitude and endurance in sickness and privation'.[19] It was well-known at the time that the upper ranks of the British Army had made several blunders in their prosecution of the war: soldiers were not given sufficiently warm clothing to withstand the freezing weather; medical care for the soldiers was poor which inspired Florence Nightingale (1820–1910)

The triumphant return of soldiers from the Crimean War as depicted in Pierce Egan the Younger's *Clifton Grey*.

to travel to the Crimea and tend to the sick. More worryingly, several strategic blunders by the army's upper ranks resulted in heavy casualties for little tactical gain – most famously the Charge of the Light Brigade, during which a regiment of cavalry was commanded to charge against an artillery battery. The tragic loss of life in this affair was commemorated by the Poet Laureate, Lord Alfred Tennyson, in *The Charge of the Light Brigade* (1854), which celebrated the soldiers' heroism.

Reynolds was more explicit with his radical beliefs than Egan, but for both of them there was little to be patriotic about. Reynolds, in his masterpiece *The Mysteries of London* (1844–48), highlighted the fact that Britain and its queen may have ruled over the greatest empire the world had ever known, but its citizens were not the beneficiaries of its vast wealth:

And in one delicious spot of that mighty city – whose thousand towers point upwards, from horizon to horizon, as an index of its boundless magnitude – stands the dwelling of one before whom all knees bow, and towards whose royal footstool none dares approach save with downcast eyes and subdued voice. The entire world showers its bounties upon the head of that favoured mortal; a nation of millions does homage to the throne whereon that being is exalted. The dominion of this personage so supremely blest extends over an empire on which the sun never sets – an empire greater than Jenghiz Khan achieved or Mohammed conquered. This is the parent of a mighty nation; and yet around that parent's seat the children crave for bread![20]

Although written in the 1840s, Reynolds's *Mysteries* was being reprinted by several publishers into the 1880s, when some of the more pro-imperial works discussed in earlier chapters were being printed. His powerful criticisms of the establishment would still have been current during the era of 'new' imperialism. Victoria in the *Mysteries* is a frivolous, flighty young woman who was at best ignorant of the plight of the poor, and if not ignorant, indifferent.[21] Prince Albert was no better: to Reynolds the Prince was little more than a useless Tory sycophant who, far from being a sponsor of social progress as the courtly newspapers would have people believe, was an oppressor of the working classes through his secret friendship with Robert Peel (1788–1850).[22] Reynolds's message was clear: the monarchy did not care for its subject peoples and the people should not reciprocate.

In such a context, why would any worker take up arms and serve his Queen and country, especially when army life was unpleasant, brutal and took men away from loved ones? In Reynolds's *The Soldier's Wife* (1852–3) the army is depicted as a service which only the most desperate or destitute men are conned to enter. At the beginning of the novel, a recruiting sergeant alights from the stagecoach in the small village of Oakley. He beguiles the young lads assembled in the local tavern with the glories of army life:

> "Talk of the hardships of a soldier's life!" said Mr Langley [the recruiting officer] ... "why it's the most beautiful state of existence that can possibly be conceived. Here you have your great lords and wealthy gentlemen paying large sums of money out of their own pocket to travel on the continent and see the fine things there; but the soldier travels to the most distant part of the earth at no expense of his own. What an honour to have your Sovereign take such an interest as to pay your travelling expenses!"[23]

The Recruiting Officer was uttering nothing more than establishment propaganda. Reynolds's novel demonstrated that the army brutalised those who served it through regular lashings; in turn, soldiers often succumbed to alcoholism to relieve their melancholy. We must also remember the context here: *The Soldier's Wife* was published at a time when the ideology of domesticity was at its height; army service takes the protagonist away from his family. The wives and children of soldiers in *The Soldier's Wife* all too often fall into poverty and in a rather dramatic turn of events, the principal character dies as a result of a harsh flogging, and the deaths of all his family members quickly follow. This was the result of doing one's duty to one's country.

An anonymously written broadside entitled *The Soldier's Catechism* from the mid-nineteenth century painted a similarly unpleasant picture of army life:

Question. What is your name?

Answer. Soldier.

Q. Who gave you that name?

A. The recruiting sergeant, when I received the enlisting shilling, whereby I was made a recruit of bayonets, bullets, and death ...

Q. Rehearse the Articles of thy Belief.

A. I believe in the Colonel Most Mighty, Maker of Sergeants and Corporals; and in his Deputy the Major, who is an officer by Commission, and rose by turn of promotion, suffered the hardships of field-service, marching and fighting; he descended into trials; after the wars he rose again; he ascended into ease, and sitteth upon the right hand of the Colonel, from whence he will come to superintend the good from the bad. I believe in the adjutant; the punishment of the guardroom; the stopping of grog; the flogging with cats; and the certainty of these things lasting. Amen.[24]

Sardonic remarks highlighting the low pay and drudgery of army life under tyrannical superior officers followed. Soldiers might think that they were fighting for the honour of their queen, country, and empire when they were sent abroad, but as Reynolds argued in one of his editorials for *Reynolds's Newspaper*, they were little more than the pawns of a capitalist oligarchy; 'a Joint Stock Company of Kings', he called them.[25]

The Chartists often had respect for Victoria herself and some of them envisaged a role for the monarchy at the head of the reconstituted political establishment for which they were campaigning – that is what they claimed anyhow. Yet when radicals of all shades appropriated patriotic language they more often than not identified loyalty to the country with a loyalty to the *people* of the nation, and most of the time they used the word 'England' or 'the English' as a synonym for Britain and the British as a whole. Theirs was a sense of patriotism that was not based on a narrow sense of loyalty to national institutions or the empire. Radical writers in Britain had always looked to America as a shining example of egalitarian democracy and Reynolds praised the people of the United

Title page to G.W.M. Reynolds's *The Soldier's Wife* which highlighted the harsh and brutal nature of army life.

States for having 'struck boldly into a sublime and wonderful path' away from the shackles of royal and imperialist despotism.[26] Reynolds, who detested British imperialism, was paradoxically very admiring of another European imperialist: Napoleon Bonaparte (1769–1821). Reynolds was a Francophile; his political beliefs were informed by the French Revolution and he saw the emperor as the embodiment of those principles. Napoleon appeared as the hero in one of Reynolds's short stories entitled *A Tale of the French Revolution*, published in *Sherwood's Monthly Miscellany* in 1838.[27] In a later novel, *Pickwick Abroad; or, The Tour in France* (1839), a similarly sympathetic depiction of the Emperor appeared.[28] Some Chartist writers likewise took inspiration from the French Revolution and the red cap of liberty was often seen at Chartist gatherings.[29]

One did not have to be a radical or a Francophile to criticise the empire or imperialists.[30] Robert Louis Stevenson, as we have seen, made few distinctions between the motivations of his respectable treasure-seekers and Long John Silver. Stevenson's *The Ebb-Tide* (1894) shows how imperialism only suited the interests of greedy white people whose lifestyles were supported by the labour of 'long-suffering natives'. While the white colonists profess to be Christians, it is evident through their actions that they are anything but Christ-like. Even colonial cheerleaders such as Rudyard Kipling criticised some aspects of imperialism. Kipling's *The Man Who Would be King* (1888) told the story of two silly colonial adventurers who go on a mission to carve out some little corner of Afghanistan where they might set themselves up as kings and live in wealth and opulence. While Kipling is obviously sympathetic to his colonialists' aims, he highlights how their greed and recklessness ultimately drives them to penury and soon death; essentially his argument is that where 'civilised' powers govern less developed people solely out of self-aggrandizing desires, then the imperialists' moral authority to govern is lost. Kipling's *Gunga Din* (1892) took aim at the often brutal treatment with which colonial officers treated their Indian servants, in spite of the fact that the servants were extremely loyal to their British sahibs. The message behind Kipling's *Gunga Din*, as with *The Man Who Would Be King*, is about the loss of British soldiers' moral authority over Indians at an individual level.

THE SOLDIER'S  CATECHISM.

Question. What is your name?
Answer. Soldier.

Q. Who gave you that name?

A. The recruiting-sergeant, when I received the enlisting shilling, whereby I was made a recruit of bayonets, bullets, and death.

Q. What did the recruiting-sergeant promise then for you?

A. He did promise and vow three things in my name. First, that I should renounce all idea of liberty, and all such nonsense. Secondly, that I should be well harassed with drill. And, thirdly, that I should stand up to be shot at whenever called upon so to do; and I heartily hope our Colonel will never call me into such a perilous position.

Q. Rehearse the Articles of thy Belief.

A. I believe in the Colonel most mighty, maker of Sergeants and Corporals; and in his deputy the Major, who is an officer by commission, and rose by turn of promotion, suffered the hardships of the field-service, marching and fighting; he descended into trials; after the wars he rose again; he ascended into ease, and sitteth on the right hand of the Colonel, from whence he will come to superintend the good from the bad. I believe in the Adjutant; the punishment of the guard-room; the stopping of grog; the flogging with cats; and the certainty of these things lasting. Amen.

Q. How many Commandments may there be?

A. Ten.

Q. What are they?

A. The same which the Colonel spake in the standing orders, saying, I am thy Colonel and commanding officer, who commands thee in the field and in quarters.

I. Thou shalt have no other Colonel but me.

II. Thou shalt not make to thyself any sergeant or corporal, that is in any European regiment above, or in any Sepoy regiment below, neither shalt thou salute them; for I thy Colonel am a jealous Colonel, and visit the iniquities of my men unto the third and fourth with stripes, and promote those who obey me and keep my standing orders.

III. Thou shalt not take the name of thy Colonel in vain, for I will not call him a good man who shall do so.

IV. Remember that thou attend church parade. Six days shalt thou have for drill and field-days; but on the seventh day thou shalt have no drill, thou, nor thy fire-lock, nor thy pouch, nor thy pouch-belt, nor thy ammunition, or any of thy appointments: for six days are sufficient for these things, and I like to rest on that day; wherefore I order church parade—attend to it.

V. Honour thy Colonel and thy Major, that thy comfort may be long in the regiment you are in.

VI. Thou shalt not get drunk on duty.

VII. Thou shalt not be absent from drill.

VIII. Thou shalt not sell thy kit.

IX. Thou shalt not come dirty to parade.

X. Thou shalt not covet thy pay-sergeants's coat, nor his place, nor his pay, nor his sword, nor his perquisites, nor his wife, nor his authority, nor any thing that is his.

Q. What do you chiefly learn by these commandments?

A. I learn two things: my duty towards my Colonel, and my duty towards my pay-sergeant.

Q. What is your duty towards your Colonel?

A. My duty towards my Colonel is to believe in him, to fear him, to obey all his orders, and all that are put in authority under him, with all my heart; to appear before him as a soldier all the days of my life; to salute him, to submit to him in all respect whatever; to put my whole trust in him, to give him thanks when he promotes me, to honour him and his commission, and to serve him as a soldier. Amen.

Q. What is your duty towards your pay-sergeant?

A. My duty towards my pay-sergeant is to attend to his directions, to look to him for pay and allowances, and all supplies of clothing; to borrow four shillings and give him five in return, to sign all books and papers he may require, and to never doubt his word in any thing.

Q. Let me hear you say your prayers.

A. Our Colonel, high in rank, honoured be thy name; may thy promotion come; thy will be done by thy sergeants, corporals, and privates. Give me my daily allowance of pay; and forgive me my crimes as I should forgive my comrade soldier. And lead me not to the triangles; but deliver me from them; and thine shall be the honour, thine the power, for ever and ever. Amen.

Q. What desirest thou in this prayer?

A. I desire my Colonel, our commanding officer, to extend his kindness to me and all my comrades; that we may honour him, serve him, and obey all his orders as we ought to do. And I pray unto him that he will be merciful unto us, and forgive us our crimes; and that he will lead us on to the defence of our country and Queen. And this I trust he will for his honour and renown; and therefore I say, Amen, and Amen.

A broadside highlighting the hardships of a soldier's life.

Punch published satires lampooning the actions of politicians and generals, as it did in the lead-up to the Second Afghan War (1878–80). Before this, Great Britain and the Russian Empire were engaged in what was effectively a cold war in which both sides sought to gain a strategic,

A scene from the Second Afghan War as depicted in Captain Brereton's *With Roberts to Candahar*.

military, or economic advantage over the other. Sometimes the tensions between the two sides boiled over into a 'hot' war, as happened in the Crimean War when Russia sought to extend its influence in Europe and the Near East at the expense of the crumbling Ottoman Empire. A peace was brokered in 1856 but the Russians continued to indirectly stir up trouble for the British.

Afghanistan had always been a buffer between the Russian Empire and British India and for this reason treaties were drawn up between Afghanistan and the two imperial powers earlier in the century in which in the Afghans promised to remain neutral, although both Britain and Russia always attempted to court the favour of Afghan rulers. In 1878 however, a new Amir named Shere-Ali ascended to power in Afghanistan. The Russians immediately sent an envoy there to curry his favour, and when the British Raj likewise sent a delegation, it was turned away. To the British, this represented a betrayal of Afghanistan's obligations to remain neutral and so war was declared.

When *Punch* covered important issues, it often included quite detailed cartoons which poked fun at the various players: in 1878 the Russian Tsar and John Bull were depicted as hunters, stalking Shere Ali whom, in a derogatory manner, was depicted as a goat. The accompanying poem then used the war-as-sport trope to highlight the pointlessness of the endeavour:

> Room enough! Yes, no doubt, and abundance of game,
> Yet the two rival sportsmen seem scarcely content.
> Fine quarries! But what if both mark down the same?
> The chance of collision 'twere hard to prevent.
> …
> Room enough! Ah! Why cannot these sportsmen agree
> To take the Earl's tip and steer clear of each other?
> If either try trespass, 'tis easy to see,
> 'Twill spoil sport and result in no end of bother![31]

The argument *Punch* was making was that all of the rivalry between the UK and Russia was simply unnecessary, and that no one wanted a war over Afghanistan. While *Punch* was critical of the tensions between Britain and Russia however, it did not amount to a rejection of imperialism. The magazine often criticised imperial policy but never called for an end to the empire itself.

Nevertheless, a war, the second one which the British fought against Afghanistan, eventually happened. The British force, commanded by Lord Roberts, was victorious in the Second Afghan War – which the Russians ultimately stayed out of – and some territory was ceded from Afghanistan to British India. After this, Roberts enjoyed some well-earned leave back in England. Yet one writer in the *Radical* scoffed at his 'victory' over the Afghans:

> General Roberts is just now having a series of grand treats throughout the country. Surely it is time some of the fuss about him ceased? After all, what has he done to merit the ovations he is receiving? Opposed to him there were no trained generals, no soldiers of military education. The Afghan generals are simply semi-barbaric chiefs of clans and tribes. The Afghans as a race are brave to recklessness, but they are badly armed, and have little or no knowledge of modern military tactics or organisation. To beat these people was no great event. No doubt General Roberts is a brave soldier and a capable officer, but the fuss about him in the country is ludicrous when his achievements are taken into consideration. A victory over distinguished generals and a trained army would be worth a nation's recognition, but to make a sensation about a general for beating a lot of disorganised tribes of half-savage hill-men is absurd, and makes England as a nation the laughing-stock of Europe.[32]

There was a still a racialist condescension towards the Afghans in *The Radical*'s comments, evident in the description of the Afghans as 'half-savage hill-men'. Yet *The Radical* journalist's comments about Lord Roberts were a stark contrast to Brereton's *With Roberts to Candahar*, in which Roberts was described as 'the hero of a hundred battles'.[33]

By the 1880s, another radical movement had emerged in Britain, many of whose writers were highly critical of imperialism: communism. The ideas espoused by Karl Marx and Friedrich Engels in *The Communist*

The famous artist, designer, and socialist activist and writer, William Morris. Although he had been through the public school system himself during their reform years, he was highly critical of imperialism.

Manifesto (1848) had far greater reach in Europe on the book's first publication than in Britain, and it would not be until 1877 that a communist organisation, named the Guild of Saint Matthew, was established in the United Kingdom. This was hardly a movement of country-wide significance however, and the first country-wide socialist organisation was the Democratic Federation, founded by a businessman named Henry Hyndman in 1881. At first it was a club for radicals of various political beliefs but in 1884 its members adopted a socialist constitution and the organisation was renamed the Social Democratic Federation. It numbered among its ranks former Chartists as well as future Labour politicians.

Communist intellectuals theorise that society progresses in stages according to changes in the means of production. These means of production are the tools which enable people to produce things, and a person's relationship to the means of production determines their class status. Societies whose economies depended upon farming, such as ancient and feudal societies, used the labour of slaves and serfs who were bound to the master or lord. In industrial societies, the working class labour for a pittance in factories producing goods for bourgeois factory owners who profit from the labour of the workers. At each stage of society there is, therefore, one dominant class and one oppressed class. The aristocracy held power in ancient and feudal societies, while the bourgeoisie held power in capitalist societies. The two classes, the ruling class and the oppressed class, were said to be in a constant state of antagonism towards each other: 'the history of all hitherto existing society is the history of class struggles', as Marx and Engels famously wrote.[34] Revolutions usually marked the transition from one stage of society to the next. The French Revolution of 1789 and the industrial revolution in Britain were said by Marx to have marked the final shift away from feudalism to capitalism and the transfer of power from the aristocracy to the bourgeoisie, whose power rested not upon land but money. Marx theorized that eventually the working class would rise up and seize the means of production from the bourgeoisie and the means of production would be placed under democratic control. After this revolution, society would effectively become classless. Socialism was originally envisioned as the transitionary phase between capitalism and communism, during which there would be a 'dictatorship of the proletariat' to ensure the implementation of a 'communal' society and defeat any attempts at counter-revolution from the bourgeoisie.

It was no coincidence that European empires emerged and established their dominance during the capitalist stage. Capitalism needs to constantly extend its reach into territories to exploit new markets. Shortly before the Russian Revolution of 1917, Lenin called imperialism 'the highest stage of capitalism'. In England, as on the continent, intellectuals began advocating a fundamental change in society along socialist lines, many of whom felt it their duty to spread socialism's message to British workers. After all, the British working class had probably been beguiled by what Marx saw as 'false-consciousness', such as patriotism, loyalty to institutions, and misplaced feelings of superiority over other races (while some members of the English socialist movement held anti–Semitic views, by and large, socialists viewed themselves as part of an internationalist movement which aimed not only to improve the condition of workers in Britain but eventually the whole world). This required an aversion to all forms of imperialism, as Ernest Belfort Bax wrote in the leading socialist journal *Commonweal* in 1885:

Markets, markets, markets! Who shall deny that this is the drone-bass ever welling up from beneath the shrill howling of "pioneers of civilisation", "avengers of national honour," "purveyors of gospel light," "restorers of order;" in short, beneath the hundred and one cuckoo cries with which the "market classes" seek to smother it or to vary its monotony? It seems well-nigh impossible there can be men so blind as not to see through these sickening hypocrisies of the governing classes, so thin as they are ... The establishment of Socialism, therefore, on any national or race basis is out of the question. No, the foreign policy of the great international Socialist party must be to break up these hideous race monopolies called empires, beginning in each case at home. Hence everything which makes for the disruption and disintegration of the empire to which he belongs must be welcomed by the Socialist as an ally. It is his duty to urge on any movement tending in any way to dislocate the commercial relations of the world, knowing that every shock the modern complex commercial system suffers weakens it and brings its destruction nearer. This is the negative side of the foreign policy of Socialism. The positive is embraced in a single sentence: to consolidate the union of the several national sections on the basis of firm and equal friendship, steadfast adherence to definite principle, and determination to present a solid front to the enemy.[35]

In this passage, Belfort Bax was demystifying the idea of the civilizing mission. There was one reason, and one reason only, that British civilisation was being spread throughout the world: capitalism. Bax's article was written while the furore was raging in parliament over whether Gordon at Khartoum should be rescued. Bax makes a veiled reference to Gordon when he states that politicians might pretend that Britain wants to make an expedition to rescue a 'Christian hero'. Yet the reason behind any rescue of Gordon is essentially the same: to secure Britain's 'market share' in that part of the world.

With William Morris (1834–96), the artist, designer and 'visionary socialist', Bax wrote a series of articles in *Commonweal* entitled 'Socialism from the Root Up'. Although Morris attended a public school, he was not a supporter of British imperialism. Instead he lent his backing to various anti-imperial causes throughout his life, such as Irish Home Rule. Ireland and Britain have had, to put it mildly, a complex and troubled history. The two nations' troubles stretch at least as far back as the Norman invasions of Ireland in the 1100s. Various English and, after 1707, British rulers, had ruled over Ireland until Morris's day. After the United Irishmen's Rebellion against British rule in 1798, the Irish parliament was disbanded, and in 1800 the country became part of the newly formed United Kingdom of Great Britain and Ireland, ruled directly from Westminster. Yet Ireland was never an equal member of this newly-forged state. It was simultaneously a colony and a member state. The majority of the Irish people, who were Catholic, were treated as an internal 'other', viewed with suspicion by the British establishment and subject to derogatory and demeaning stereotypes in popular culture and economic and social marginalisation. In Morris's time, some Liberal Party members supported Home Rule for Ireland, hoping to stem the tide of Irish nationalist agitation which saw Anglo-Irish landlords' properties attacked, and isolated acts of terrorism. Gladstone's Home Rule Bill in the 1880s, which would have given Ireland its own parliament, was opposed by politicians on the more conservative side for two reasons: it would have politically marginalised Ulster Protestants in a predominantly Catholic country, and it was not fair for a devolved Ireland to be required to contribute to a UK-wide budget with no representation in Westminster. Morris turned his attention to the matter in his writings.

That Ireland should be ruled by the Irish was beyond doubt, and this change, in Morris's view, should be brought about ideally by a revolution. He wrote in *Commonweal* in 1885, 'we revolutionists rejoice in it [Irish Revolution] on those grounds, and in the blow which it will deal at the great Bourgeois Power – the British Empire.'[36] As an internationalist Morris was however concerned about the narrow nationalist focus of the cause of Irish independence:

> If only the Irish could take this lesson to heart, and make up their minds that even if they have to wait for it, their revolution shall be part of the great international movement; they will then be rid of all the foreigners that they want to be rid of. For my part I do not believe in the race-hatred of the Irish against the English: they hate their English *masters*, and well they may; and their English masters are now trying hard to stimulate the race-hatred among their English brethren, the workers, by all this loud talk of the integrity of the Empire and so forth. But when once the Irish people have got rid of their masters, Irish and English both, there will, I repeat, be no foreigners to hate in Ireland, and she will look back at the present struggle for mere nationality as a nightmare of the charmed sleep in which Landlordism and Capitalism have held her so long, as they have other nations. To the Irish, therefore, as to all other nations, whatever their name and race, we Socialists say, your revolutionary struggles will be abortive or lead to mere disappointment unless you accept as your watchword,
>
> WAGE-WORKERS OF ALL COUNTRIES UNITE![37]

For the Irish to be truly free, Morris thought, they had to be free of the tyranny of capitalism, should abandon their hatred towards their English masters, and focus on building socialism.[38]

Morris had a vision of what a future socialist Britain would look like in *News from Nowhere; or, An Epoch of Rest* (1890). It is the story of a gentleman who, having been to an evening lecture at a Socialist League meeting, finds himself pondering what would happen on the morning of the revolution during his ride home on the London underground, which Morris amusingly calls 'a vapour bath of hurried and discontented

THIS IS THE PICTURE OF THE OLD HOUSE BY THE THAMES TO WHICH THE PEOPLE OF THIS STORY WENT. HEREAFTER FOLLOWS THE BOOK IT-SELF WHICH IS CALLED NEWS FROM NOWHERE OR AN EPOCH OF REST & IS WRITTEN BY WILLIAM MORRIS.

William Morris's *News from Nowhere; or, An Epoch of Rest* (1886) sees a time traveller from Victorian London awaken after the year 2003 when the world has become a communist utopia, 'the epoch of rest'. The book was highly critical of imperialism, which many late-Victorian communists viewed as an extension of capitalism, and soldiers such as General Gordon.

humanity, a carriage of the underground railway' – a tube ride back then could be as hot and unpleasant as it can today.[39] He sits in the carriage thinking of the revolution and mutters to himself: 'if I could but see a day of it ... if I could but see it!'[40] In the morning he wakes up in London sometime after the year 2003. Britain has been transformed into a socialist utopia when the rule of masters has given way to fellowship as a result of a revolution in 1950s. Now, in 2003, people work for subsistence and to help others, not to please some capitalist overlord. An 'epoch of rest' from capitalist wage slavery has been ushered in. The Victorian gentleman is surprised when a boatman refuses to accept payment for taking him across the river.[41] Cash and coins are a quaint relic of a bygone era for the people of Britain in 2003, fit only for a museum. There was no place for imperialism in *News from Nowhere*. The so-called heroes of the British Empire were simply brutes whose only interest was in extending the reaches of capitalism, as one of the future-dwellers reveals to the time traveller:

When the civilised World-Market coveted a country not yet in its clutches some transparent pretext was found – the suppression of a slavery different from, and not so cruel, as that of commerce; the pushing of a religion no longer believed in by its promoters; the 'rescue' of some desperado or homicidal madman whose misdeeds had got him into trouble amongst the natives of the 'barbarous' country – any stick, in short, which would beat the dog at all. Then some bold, unprincipled, ignorant adventurer was found (no difficult task in the days of competition), and he was bribed to 'create a market' by breaking up whatever traditional society there might be in the doomed country, and by destroying whatever leisure or pleasure he found there. He forced wares on the natives which they did not want, and took their natural products in 'exchange', as this form of robbery was called, and thereby he 'created new wants', to supply which (that is, to be allowed to live by their new masters) the hapless helpless people had to sell themselves into the slavery of hopeless toil so that they might have something wherewith to purchase the nullities of 'civilisation.'[42]

Morris criticised a lot of the things about the British Empire which its cheerleaders had lauded: 'the suppression of slavery' refers to the slavery of Africans, abolished in Britain in 1833. Some of the Royal Navy's resources after that date were indeed put to use in combatting the transportation of slaves from other nations. But for Morris, while the empire had helped put an end to African slavery, imperialism perpetuated slavery of a different kind: capitalist wage slavery. People in the 1890s still toiled in factories for a pittance and nothing had improved for the working class. Other socialist journalists made similar points: when a correspondent for *The Social Democrat* interviewed a 97-year-old Chartist in 1897 named 'Rex', as Rex detailed his life of perpetual poverty, the writer exclaimed, 'And it was Britain who freed the Blacks!'[43]

Morris's placing of the word 'barbarous' in quotation is meant to be read as sardonic; it was not the 'natives' who were barbarous but the aforementioned 'desperados', 'homicidal madmen', and 'ignorant adventurers'; those same military heroes who featured in contemporary light fiction and popular biographies, such as Gordon, Roberts, and Clive. Annie Besant, the socialist, feminist activist, and advocate of Indian home rule, took aim at Clive in *England, India, and Afghanistan* (1878), and called him

A turbulent and ill-conditioned boy, the torment of Market Drayton, his native town, the despair of his family, who had been joyfully shipped up to India as a writer in the Company's service, and thus got rid of, flung down his pen, caught up his sword, pleaded to be sent on active service, and was given 200 English soldiers and 300 Sepoys, flung himself and his little army against Arcot [the Siege of Arcot in the Carnatic Wars] in a storm of thunder and lightning, took it by surprise from its startled and panic-stricken garrison, and entrenched himself in his captured stronghold.[44]

But what did Besant say of Clive's glorious victories in India?

Glorious? Oh, yes! If glory means burning towns, slaughtered men, ravished women, murdered children, desolated fields, fire-blackened houses; if murder and rapine and gigantic robbery and fraud be crimes, the glories of Clive lie only in the vastness of infamy.[45]

HENRY M. STANLEY.

Yet were not these men motivated by religious convictions? Were they not warriors of Christ and the empire? *Reynolds's Newspaper*, much like other newspapers, often reviewed popular history books as well as fictional works. These were the reviewer's comments on Besant's book:

Mrs. Besant has published this work with the obvious purpose of showing how might has been made to trample on the right in reference to English policy in Indian affairs. She shows

H. M. Stanley who, along with David Livingstone, 'infested' Africa.

how force and fraud have gained for us the upper hand in India, and probably thinks, with ourselves, that so long as we continue in the same way coveting, seizing, and appropriating to ourselves

PIONEERS OF CIVILISATION
THE MEETING OF LIVINGSTONE AND STANLEY IN CENTRAL AFRICA.

the territories of others, it might be as well to dispense with the presence of missionaries in India. For it would be absurd to believe the native mind so obscure as not to discover the startling contrast in the teachings of the Bible and those who proclaim it to be the text-book of their conduct in all things.[46]

Imperialists' appropriation of Christianity as a mere pretext for spreading capitalism's tentacles into unspoiled native societies was a point also raised in *Reynolds's Newspaper* in 1894 who said that 'the missionary enterprise of this country is merely an agency for the extension of "the Empire" – that is, of British civilization; in other words, of British shoddy goods'.[47] (G. W. M. Reynolds, the proprietor of *Reynolds's Newspaper*, was not a socialist or anti-capitalist, although his paper took a leftward turn towards the end of the century).

Imperial heroes' Christian morality was, in William Morris's eyes, nothing but a pretext for extending the reaches of capitalism and ruining the culture of native societies. Morris even took aim at the missionaries David Livingstone and H.M. Stanley, whom he said 'infested' Africa. The comment was very topical as, when Morris wrote those words, Stanley had just returned from his third African expedition and was advocating for further colonization to help civilize the Africans.

While William Morris held anti-imperialist views, some socialists, while not endorsing capitalism and imperialism, viewed the empire as a means through which humanity might be lifted out of oppression. James Ramsay MacDonald, who later served as prime minister, argued as such in *Labour and the Empire* (1907) and said that while imperialism in its early days was abhorrent to democrats, the emergence of many formerly subject regions as self-governing dominions was now acceptable to democratic parties, and that Labour's ultimate aim should be to use the empire to create a better, more egalitarian world.[48]

If another nation should make war upon Britain and its empire, then the editor of the leading Marxist newspaper *The Clarion*, Robert Blatchford (1851–1943), proudly declared that

England's enemies are my enemies. I am an Englishman. That is the point I want to make clear. I am not a jingo, I am opposed to war. I do not approve of this present war [the Boer War]. But I cannot go with those Socialists whose sympathies are with the enemy. My whole heart is with the British troops ... I am for peace and international brotherhood. But when England is at war I'm English.

Blatchford counted himself as both a socialist and a patriot: 'I am ready to sacrifice socialism for the sake of England, but never to sacrifice England for the sake of socialism,' he once said. He was fiercely proud of his English heritage and claimed that his own brand of socialism had nothing to do with Marx but was inspired by earlier English writings on collective ownership stretching from the teachings of John Ball (d. 1381) and thence to the Diggers.[49] Blatchford's position nevertheless provoked debate in the socialist press. Throughout the nineteenth century, Britain gradually extended its hold over South Africa. By 1877, the British controlled almost the entire region save for two independent Boer republics located inside it: the Orange Free State and the Transvaal Republic. The British had approached the leaders of these small republics with the aim of creating a federal South Africa which would be modelled on the same lines as Canada. This proposal was rejected however, and ultimately two wars would have to be fought against this rag-tag bunch of farmers. The question for many socialists remained: who was worse – the British or the Boers? Even non-socialist writers had contempt for the Boers, in particular over their treatment of black people, whom they kept in a state of near slavery.[50] Here we had that great bourgeois power, the British Empire, waging war upon a poorer people. Yet these victims also treated other workers – black people – with contempt.

The socialist Irish Republican hero of the Easter Rising, James Connolly (1868–1916), hit back against Blatchford and was heavily critical of his socialist colleagues who viewed Britain as somehow exceptional and not as exploitative as other empires:

As Socialists – and therefore anxious to at all times to throw the full weight of whatever influence we possess upon the side of the forces making most directly for Socialism – we have often been somewhat disturbed in our mind by observing in the writings and speeches of some of our foreign comrades a tendency to discriminate in favour of Great Britain in all the international complications in which that country may be involved over questions of territorial annexation, spheres of influence, etc., in barbarous or semi-civilised portions of the globe.[51]

Ideas about civilisation and barbarism and the superiority of white-skinned people are obviously culturally ingrained in Connolly's political philosophy, and this comes through in his speech.

The Boer question, indeed, seemed to have divided socialists just as it divided British society as a whole, especially when the unpleasant news filtered back home that British forces had interned Boer women and children in concentration camps. Through the whole of the Victorian period therefore, the British Empire and the actions of its soldiers and administrators were never endorsed by the whole population and there were competing ideas about imperialism and its proponents printed in the press.

Conclusion: Heroes No More

Lytton Strachey's chief mission, of course, was to take down once and for all the pretensions of the Victorian age to moral superiority... neither the Americans nor the English have ever, since *Eminent Victorians* appeared, been able to feel quite the same about the legends that had dominated their pasts. Something had been punctured for good.

Edmund Wilson, *The New Republic* (1932)

At the beginning of chapter one, Matthew Prior's *Solomon* was quoted in which he extolled the glorious rise of the British Empire, whose power stretched from pole to pole and whose ships unfurled their sails across the oceans. Yet as early as 1718, Prior foresaw what would eventually happen:

> Rever'd and happy, she shall long remain
> Of human things least changeable, least vain;
> Yet all must with the general doom comply,
> And this great glorious power, though last, must die.

All empires fall eventually. In the twentieth century, Britain's name would soon be added to that list of great fallen civilizations and empires which included Babylon, Persia, Rome, Byzantium, Spain, and Portugal. Writers in the new century were aware that Britain's empire and world influence were fading. G.W.M. Reynolds died in 1879 but *Reynolds's Newspaper* lived on and in July 1900, an interesting article was printed in the paper entitled 'The Tottering Empire'. Capitalism and greed had brought an empire, which might have been a force for good in the world, to the brink of disaster. It entrenched the power of a ruling class at home and abroad who felt no obligation to do any good for their subject citizens

A satire from *Punch*'s September 1892 issue on imperial entrepreneur, Cecil Rhodes, who has always been a controversial figure.

but tax them for the privilege of maintaining 'this bastard empire'. The civilising mission was just a shallow pretext for making money. The soldiers of the empire ought to be in gaol. In the paper's reflection upon the recent reverses of the British army's fortunes in the Boer War, it was clear that even the prestige of the British army was no longer what it once was. The empire was rotten and it was falling.[1]

However, the British Empire took a while to fall. The First World War broke out in 1914; as Andrew Thompson points out, there is some evidence in the memoirs of mid-twentieth century politicians which suggests that their youthful readings of Henty books were influential in encouraging them to sign up for the army. After the slaughter and mass bodily dismemberment of what was quite a senseless war – and the death of many of the officer class who came from the public schools – it would have made sense to writers to have abandoned imperialist ideology altogether. Yet reprints of Henty's works continued to be popular into the early twentieth century as did stories of colonial adventures. H. Rider Haggard continued to publish widely-read works. He was an average writer but he knew the public liked tales of adventure and, realising he was on to a good thing, decided to resurrect both Allan and Ayesha in successive novels. Yet in some of Haggard's later novels, criticisms of imperialism appeared.[2] In *Allan Quatermain*, the eponymous hero muses upon the concept of 'civilisation' and 'savagery', and rubbishes the idea of white racial superiority.[3] In his sequel to *She*, Ayesha declares that she shall descend upon the world and come to the aid of those oppressed by capitalism and warfare the world over by purifying mankind:

> "Why not?" she asked. "It would be more simple and bring them closer to the time when they were good and knew not luxury and greed."
>
> "And smashed in each other's heads with stone axes," added Leo.
>
> "Who now pierce each other's hearts with steel, or those leaden missiles of which thou hast told me. Oh! Leo, when the nations are beggared and their golden god is down; when the usurer and the fat merchant tremble and turn white as chalk because their hoards are but useless dross; when I have made the bankrupt Exchanges of the world my mock, and laugh across the ruin of its richest markets, why, then, will not true worth come to its heritage again?"[4]

(Although nominally a Tory, in later life, Rider Haggard realised that his thinking on economic and social matters was out-of-step with mainstream

Watercolour of Ottawa in the early twentieth century. Canada was granted *de facto* independence from the British Empire in 1867. To this day the country remains in the Commonwealth of Nations.

Conservative thought).[5] He continued to write, and even though none of his novels were ground-breaking and mostly rehashes of his usual 'lost world' plots, his works continued to be enjoyed by younger readers into the 1940s and provided material for entertaining films as well.[6]

Other new novels appeared which mimicked 'Hentyesque' fiction from the previous century. C.S. Forester's *Hornblower*, set during the Napoleonic Wars, told the adventures of a naval officer named Horatio Hornblower. Hornblower is a middle-class lad sent to sea and serves as a midshipman before rising through the navy's ranks and becoming commander of a 74-gun ship of the line. He participates in famous campaigns and meets historical figures such as Captain Edward Pellew (1757–1833). Throughout the series, Hornblower manifests many of the public school traits that readers expected of imperial warriors. When we first meet Hornblower as a lowly midshipman on HMS *Lydia*, the crew have had very little excitement for many months. Yet rather than remain idle, Hornblower 'exercises himself for an hour each morning'.[7] He is, of course, fervently loyal to England, and is the ultimate gentleman. In one of the later novels, Forester takes the idea of a gentleman's honour to an almost absurd end; Hornblower is captured as a prisoner of war by the Spanish and, even though he gets the chance to escape, stays in his prison because he gave the Spanish gaoler his *parole* that he would not attempt it. This highly improbable plotline was then reproduced in the moderately successful TV series which aired in the early 2000s.

While the empire seemed as strong as ever in the realm of light fiction, in real life, as *Reynolds's Newspaper* foresaw in 1900, it was indeed 'tottering' in spite of being enlarged with the addition of League of Nations mandate territories in 1919 (mandate territories were mostly in the Middle East and included Palestine and Mesopotamia, which formerly belonged to the Ottoman Empire which collapsed in the First World War's aftermath). The journalist and imperial ideologue Sir Archibald Hurd complained that Canada – a self-governing dominion – was rarely supportive of the mother country's foreign policy.[8] Ireland achieved its independence from Britain in 1922 with the signing of the Anglo-Irish Treaty after Irish freedom fighters had fought a bloody civil war, although the predominantly Protestant northern part of the island opted to remain part of the United Kingdom.

To celebrate the 'greatness' of the British Empire, the government decided in 1924 that a British Empire Exhibition would be held at Wembley in a purpose-built Empire Stadium. It was hoped that the event would foster a sense of loyalty to the empire among the British public. This spectacle was necessary because the empire faced competition for economic and military supremacy from the United States. The public in the 1920s also seemed less enthusiastic in maintaining imperialism than their Victorian forebears. Ticket sales were low and the exhibition was a financial flop. When the authorities ran a second season in May 1925 – all the more necessary to recoup the financial loss from the first event – some of the colonial authorities were reluctant to participate. There was no official participation at the second event by the government of India. The 1924 exhibition may have wanted to present the empire as 'a Family of Nations' but it was looking as though it was an increasingly dysfunctional one.

While adventure novels were popular, soon the decline of imperial loyalty among the reading public would be reflected in literature. While writers such as Reynolds and Morris, who had spoken out against British imperialism, might have intensely disliked some of the leading men of the empire, there was in their writings some of that characteristic Victorian self-restraint which perhaps prevented them from firing full literary broadsides against their subjects on a personal level. This was not so with writers from the twentieth century. The First World War, while it did not immediately sound the death-knell of the imperial hero in popular culture, seemed to have made British society a bit less deferential to the previous century's 'eminent Victorians'. This attitude was brilliantly articulated by Lytton Strachey in *Eminent Victorians* (1918), a collection of brief biographies of four leading lights of the Victorian era: Cardinal Manning, Florence Nightingale, Thomas Arnold, and General Gordon. Arnold and Manning's character flaws were focused upon in Strachey's work, but the surprising inclusion in the book for a modern reader is Florence Nightingale.[9] Who could possibly find anything objectionable in the character of the saintly 'Lady with the Lamp' who tended to the sick during the Crimean War? Yet Strachey argued that 'the Miss Nightingale of fact was not as facile as fancy painted her … in the real Miss Nightingale … there was also less that was agreeable'.[10] Her 'disagreeable' nature was evinced by the fact that she was an unsparing demon towards the nurses who worked under her: 'her virtue had dwelt in hardness, and she had poured forth her unstinted usefulness with a bitter smile upon her lips'.[11] However, Strachey's most venomous criticism was directed at General Gordon, in whose soul, he argued, dwelt the spirit

Watercolour of Government House in India during the early twentieth century. After India and Pakistan won their independence, this building became the residence of the Indian President.

of ambition, egotism, and self-righteousness, all of which was the result of an unhinged devotion to his own peculiar Christian creed, which contradicted the peaceable teachings of Christ:

> He was an English gentleman, an officer, a man of energy and action, a lover of danger and the audacities that defeat danger; a passionate creature, flowing over with the self-assertiveness of independent judgment and the arbitrary temper of command. Whatever he might find in his pocket-Bible … what he did find was that the Will of God was inscrutable and absolute; that it was man's duty to follow where God's hand led; and, if God's hand led towards violent excitements and extraordinary vicissitudes, that it was not only futile, it was impious to turn another way.[12]

Strachey was a founding member of the Bloomsbury Group, a mixture of artists, writers, literary critics, and even economists who met in the reading rooms of the British Museum to discuss literary and philosophical topics. They were liberals who desired to cast off the Victorian and Edwardian social *moeurs* with which they were raised – which stressed respectability, public virtue and achievement, and sexual propriety – and embrace a different, more liberalised and 'modern' lifestyle. Strachey's *Eminent Victorians*, then, represented a clash between the ideals of modernism and Victorianism. The American literary critic Edmund Wilson remarked that Strachey had once-and-for-all destroyed the reputation of the military hero in the public eye.[13]

Where Strachey took aim at soldiers like Gordon, his friend and fellow Bloomsbury Group member E.M. Forster (1879–1970) highlighted the injustices committed by imperial bureaucrats in *A Passage to India* (1924). The novel exposed the racial tensions between the British ruling class and their Indian subjects when young Dr Aziz is accused of raping Miss Adela Quested while visiting the fictional Marabar Caves. The charges turn out to be unfounded but Aziz, who had been largely indifferent to the English presence in India before the trial, begins to resent them afterwards.

It is worth dwelling here on the character of Ronny Heaslop, a city magistrate and Adela's fiancé. Ronny is the product of the Edwardian public school system, imbued with all his class's racial prejudices. He views the Indians either as childlike or potentially criminal subjects who need to be kept in check, as he says in conversation with Mrs Moore:

> "We're not out here for the purpose of behaving pleasantly!" [said Ronny]
> "What do you mean?" [replied Mrs Moore]
> "What I say. We're out here to do justice and keep the peace."
> "Them's my sentiments. India isn't a drawing room."
> "Your sentiments are those of a god," she said quietly, but it was his manner rather than his sentiments that annoyed her. Trying to recover his temper, he said, "India likes gods."
> "And Englishmen like posing as gods."[14]

The fact that Ronny views himself as being in India for the sole purpose of 'doing justice' and 'keeping the peace' suggests that he does not actually believe in the imperial civilising mission. India in Forster's novel is now, in effect, a colony which people such as Ronny have been given the 'task' of running in an orderly manner because they have essentially been 'stuck with' it, so to speak. There is no grand vision for the so-called improvement of the country as there was in earlier works when British philanthropists wanted to 'civilise' India. Now all that exists in the subcontinent – at least how it is portrayed in the novel – is the British ruling class and its civil service, their princely state lackeys, and the subjugated Indian populace.

Were Ronny a real person, he would have found himself out of a job by the late 1940s. After the Second World War the Labour Party swept to power in Britain in a landslide victory and began the process of decolonisation, continued by successive Conservative governments. In rapid succession, a number of colonies were granted independence from Britain. India gained independence on 15 August 1947 but it was anything but a peaceful 'transfer of power'. Thomas Macauley wanted to create a class of educated and westernised Indians who, he hoped, would improve the subcontinent and remake it in England's image; it was primarily members of this educated middle-class, such as Mahatma Gandhi (1869–1948), Jawaharlal Nehru (1889–1964), and Muhammed

Ali Jinnah (1876–1948), who eventually turned on the British and led the charge for independence in the twentieth century.

The British divided the subcontinent into two nations: India and Pakistan. The establishment of the latter was to allay India's Muslims' fears that, after independence, they would be discriminated against in what was a majority-Hindu country. Lord Mountbatten (1900–79), the last viceroy, oversaw the partition of the subcontinent, which led to one of the largest scenes of mass-migration in modern times. Hindus in what is now Pakistan made the journey to India and Muslims in India attempted to get to Pakistan. Not all of the estimated 14 million people who set out to their respective destinations survived the journey. The partition of the country led to horrific scenes of intra-ethnic violence between Muslims, Hindus, and Sikhs. For three hundred years, the British had pursued a policy of 'divide and rule' in India, stoking resentment between Muslims, Hindus, and Sikhs. That policy now bore its ugly fruit. With the partition of the country looming, people of different religions, who had formerly been neighbours and good friends, committed horrific acts of violence against each other. There are reports of trains arriving at stations containing nothing but bloody corpses while men fought in the streets with any weapons they could find. The worst atrocities were committed against women and children. Many women of both Hindu and Muslim origin were stripped naked in the streets and publicly humiliated, while some women's breasts were sliced off and others had their wombs cut open. Some of the women who survived their ordeal were killed by their fathers for the sake of their family's honour. Those families who made it to the other side found often themselves homeless and penniless in their newly adopted countries.

Burma and Sri Lanka gained independence in 1948; Libya was freed from British rule in 1951, while various other African colonies such as Sudan, Ghana, Somalia, Nigeria, Sierra Leone, Tanzania, Uganda, Kenya, Malawi, Zambia, Gambia, Botswana, Lesotho, Mauritius, and Swaziland, received their independence over the next two decades. Most of these newly-independent nations remained in the Commonwealth of Nations, which is a relatively benign – compared to the empire at any rate – if rather pointless supranational entity and membership of it has little relevance for the inhabitants of its constituent member states. One could be forgiven for thinking that it was maintained in the post-war period only as a consolation for the UK's loss of the empire and a tonic for politicians reeling from Britain's decline from great power status.

Another such 'tonic' was the Festival of Britain, held in London in 1951. The event was intended to commemorate a hundred years since the Great Exhibition of 1851, when Britain was 'the workshop of the world'. Britain was obviously much a different country by 1951 however: the UK was war-damaged and near bankrupt. The new festival therefore aimed to foster a sense of national pride by celebrating British achievements in art, science, and technology. While various Commonwealth countries were invited to participate in the event, most refused to send representatives because they were now proud independent nations and there seemed to be little point in taking part in an event which looked as though it would rehash the same ideas of British cultural superiority found in times gone by.

In political terms, Britain was no longer a superpower but it took the international humiliation of the Suez Crisis in 1956 for its ruling class to realise this fact. Britain had, on paper at least, granted independence to Egypt in 1922. Yet it was a shallow independence: the British maintained a strong military and diplomatic presence in Cairo because the Suez Canal was central to Britain's military needs as it provided a much shorter route for ships to travel through Egypt to India than having to go all the way around Africa. Right up the 1950s, British capitalists were the majority shareholders in the Suez Canal Company but the Egyptians had little respect for the British puppets who ran their country. In 1952, the Egyptians had had enough: under Colonel Nasser's leadership, the Egyptian monarchy was overthrown and a republic was established. Nasser caused the British, French, Israeli, and US governments much concern for he was rather too friendly towards the Soviet Union. The final straw for the British, French, and Israelis came in 1956 when Nasser decided to nationalise the canal without consulting any of the Western powers. Feeling that their prestige had been damaged, Britain, France, and Israel launched an invasion of Egypt on 29 October.

Military intervention turned out to be a big mistake: although the operation was successful, at an international level, Britain, France, and Israel were seen as the aggressors. Unusually for the time, the USA and the Soviet Union stood together and condemned the action at a meeting of the UN Security Council. After all, the Americans could not on the one hand condemn Soviet intervention in Hungary and simultaneously sanction British, French, and Israeli actions in Egypt.[15] Besides, if the USA supported action against Egypt, that might push the whole Arab world into the Soviet sphere of influence. It truly was a changed world: no longer could former colonial powers such as Britain and France strut about on the world stage invading countries with no regard for international public opinion as they had done in the past. If it had not been clear before the Suez Crisis, the international reaction to it put in sharp relief Britain's decline as a world power, and the Prime Minister, Anthony Eden (1897–1977), was forced to resign over the matter.

A film entitled *Sammy Going South* (1963) – named *A Boy Ten Feet Tall* in the USA – was set during the Suez Crisis. Young Sammy, a British boy, lives with his parents in Port Said when the French and

Watercolour of Kingston, Jamaica. After independence, many former British colonies and dominions opted to remain within the British Commonwealth (now simply 'Commonwealth'). Some countries such as Jamaica even retained the British monarch as their head of state.

British forces begin their invasion. His parents are tragically killed in the bombing and he has to fend for himself in Egypt. This was hardly a ringing endorsement of British foreign policy. Yet the film does hark back to some of the older motifs found in Victorian fiction. The actor who played Sammy, Fergus McLelland, was chosen by the producers because he looked athletic and like he might be able to survive in such a situation: 'He was a lean, hard, little boy. Tough as old nails ... a really strong character', the producers maintained. Alone in a country that is understandably hostile to the British at this point, he resolves to make the 2,000 mile trek south to Durban in South Africa where his aunt resides. The film is a fusion of the picaresque and the *Bildungsroman* (this German word is the name for a genre of fiction dealing with a youth's formative years, education, and character development): Sammy 'toughens up' during the many scrapes he gets into on the way, during which he meets an array of weird and wonderful characters, including an Arab tradesman and a diamond smuggler who is very 'Quatermainesque' (if I may coin a word). After he is reunited with his aunt, he finds out that the diamond smuggler has left him his treasure, meaning that from then on he will be able to live like a gentleman, which is not totally dissimilar to the plots of earlier imperial tales.

In the 1950s even the image of the good and 'civilised' upper-class schoolboy was criticised. In William Golding's *Lord of the Flies* (1954) a group of preparatory school boys are marooned on a tropical island and, at first, they try to establish a society which mirrors the British one which they knew back home. However, the posh boys quickly turn into violent little savages when a lad called Jack takes command. Jack becomes a petty tyrant who sanctions the torture some of the other boys who do not conform to his worldview. Interestingly, the most likeable character in the whole novel is a boy called Piggy. He is not like the other lads and comes from a humbler, less affluent background. He is the voice of reason in the novel and generally kind but he is viewed as an outcast by others. Piggy is eventually killed by Roger, one of Jack's henchmen and, as the one character who held on to his humanity and decency, his death symbolises the boys' ultimate descent into savagery. When a naval officer finally disembarks on the island and finds the children, he is shocked that young British boys – the cream of the crop of upper middle-class youths – could have acted in such a way. As Golding shows, ideas of 'civilisation', honour, decency, as depicted in countless earlier Victorian and Edwardian novels, were largely superficial. In the previous century, it was always the sons of the upper classes who had the starring role in adventure novels and were held up by writers as characters from whom young working-class readers could take moral instruction. This was not the case in Golding's novel.

This is not to say that every single aspect of late-Victorian imperialist ideology died a death in culture at large. It had always been the case that older ideas of quintessential English behaviour were simply adapted to serve the needs of imperialist ideology. The idea of the Englishman's innate sense of fair play was far older than the era of 'new' imperialism; the empire never eclipsed loyalty to the nation and monarchy, and the accession of a new queen at the height of decolonisation, who would not be styled 'Empress', meant that popular patriotism could be refocused back onto the nation state. In the public schools, athleticism was promoted originally, not with specifically imperial concerns in mind, but with the aim of building good Christian gentlemen. And athleticism lives on in popular culture: all the heroic characters in movies are fit and healthy and often look superhuman. Finally, because fair play was never strictly imperialist, the quality continued to play a part in fictional works right until the 1950s. Fair play was called one of the key British values by Gordon Brown as recently as 2008.

In popular culture there remains a rather complex enthusiasm for the days of the empire and imperialism. During the era of decolonisation in the 1960s, the image of a toff in a pith helmet and redcoat was lampooned spectacularly by the predominantly working-class cast of *Carry On Up the Khyber*. The film does, however, rehearse many colonial tropes such as devious Indians seeking to overthrow the British rulers, and the film does not feature any Indian person in any of its major roles. *Carry On Up the Khyber* should be seen as a satire on the eccentricities of the British imperial ruling class, its bumbling absent-minded approach to rule, its sham stoicism and its stiff upper lip mentality, rather than as a criticism of the empire itself.

This was also the era of movies such as *Zulu* (1964) in which the tale of a small band of British soldiers fighting off hordes of Zulu warriors is portrayed as heroic. Even seemingly non-imperial figures such as James Bond – an upper-class, privately educated secret agent who speaks the Queen's English – is really just an imperial throwback who, through his actions, proves that Britain is still a major power to be reckoned with in a post-imperial age. As Matthew Parker points out, Bond's creator, the novelist Ian Fleming, was a man of the empire: he lived in Jamaica and 'he could see the changes happening in Jamaica as British power crumbled. And he wasn't happy about it.' Much like a Victorian adventurer, through being fit and strong Bond is able to get out of any scrape; he is decent and honourable yet his enemies are not and it is in this sense that he is a colonial-era throwback. Contemporary films such as *Viceroy's House*, which is nothing but a hagiography of Mountbatten and his wife Edwina, and *Victoria and Abdul*, likewise demonstrate that the nostalgia for a golden age of British imperialism remains strong among the cinema-going public.

Something of Jack Harkaway remains in George MacDonald's Fraser's *Flashman* novels. The character of Henry Flashman originally appeared in Thomas Hughes's novel *Tom Brown's Schooldays* (1857), which tells the story of Tom Brown who attends Rugby school under the tutelage of Dr Arnold. Flashman was the school bully in Hughes's novel and was depicted as one of those 'old-school', pre-Arnoldian types of public school pupils who spent his days drinking, for which is expelled at the end of the story. Fraser gave Flashman a rehabilitation: as in the Victorian stories of old, Flashman finds himself in the army and takes part in some famous battles from British imperial history, but he is not brave and heroic like the heroes of Henty books and on some occasions flees the battlefield. MacDonald Fraser did not tinker with the values of Hughes's original Flashman too much. Fraser's Flashman is a compulsive womaniser whose chief 'virtues' are 'horses, languages, and fornication'.[16] Yet much like the pirate characters of literature, readers cannot help but like him.

Allan Quatermain's spirit survives in the popular Indiana Jones series of films. The ridiculous plot of *Raiders of the Lost Ark* (1981) sees Dr Jones, an academic, recruited by the US military to prevent the Nazis gaining possession of the long-lost Ark of the Covenant which they believe will imbue their army with supernatural power and make them unstoppable. Just as Quatermain embodied a spirit of rough British heroism in the

1800s, Jones encapsulates a spirit of American self-reliance, daring, and bravery in overcoming insurmountable odds. Owing to the success of the Indiana Jones movies, a version of *King Solomon's Mines* was produced in 1985 starring Richard Chamberlain in the role of Allan Quatermain; it enjoyed enough success at the box office to justify the production of a sequel in 1986 entitled *Allan Quatermain and the Lost City of Gold*. These were but pale imitations of Indiana Jones however; Chamberlain's Quatermain was indistinguishable from Indiana Jones, dressed in a khaki shirt and wearing a brown hat.

The reputation of Robert Clive has certainly taken a hammering in the twentieth century. William Dalrymple argued recently that Clive was 'an unstable psychopath' and that the men of the East India Company were 'the original corporate raiders'.[17] The Company was recently represented in the BBC series *Taboo* (2017) as a sinister, secretive organisation similar to the NSA in the US today: rich and powerful, with members of the government in its pocket – it was certainly not a wholly inaccurate portrayal of the 'honourable' Company.

In 2002, additionally, activists from London's Sikh community wanted the name of Havelock Road in London changed because it was a constant and painful reminder of the atrocities committed by Henry Havelock who 'killed so many innocent people who were protesting against the British Raj'.[18] Two years earlier, the then London Mayor, Ken Livingstone had argued that Havelock's statue in Trafalgar Square should be taken down because it no longer represented the values of a progressive, modern United Kingdom.

The furore around Havelock's statue would not be the last time that campaigners fought for the removal of certain monuments. Many of the Victorian era's leading lights studied at Oxford University because, along with Cambridge University, the institution was seen as a place where the public schoolboy and future imperial servant finished his education. After they got rich on the spoils of empire, many Victorian imperialists left money in their wills to Oxbridge colleges. Cecil Rhodes (1853–1902) left an endowment which provided financial assistance to scholars from Zimbabwe to study at Oxford, and in 2016 Oxford found itself at the centre of a controversy when students campaigned for a statue of Rhodes which adorned the front of Oriel College to be taken down.

The #RhodesMustFall hashtag campaign was started on Twitter and the movement's leaders suggested that the fact that the statue was still standing was yet another sign that Britain had not yet come to terms with its colonial past or apologised for the actions of 'heroes' such as Cecil Rhodes. Some conservative commentators in the press invoked the now tedious accusation that the campaigners were simply 'snowflake' students who were silly to have been 'triggered' by a statue. Meanwhile, parts of the liberal press, such as the *Guardian*, were broadly in agreement with the aims of the campaigners.

It is not only in the modern period that Rhodes has become a divisive figure however. It is doubtful whether the Victorians ever viewed him in a favourable light at all, and 2016 was not the first time that Oxford University found itself in the middle of a Rhodes-related controversy. When the university conferred the honorary degree of Doctor of Civil Laws on him in 1899, a number of academics signed a letter of protest to the university authorities, claiming that a man whose actions and views were controversial should never have been given such an honour. After the ceremony, he was greeted with derision from the undergraduates,[19] while satirical poems that were highly critical of him circulated in left-wing newspapers.[20] Rhodes was never the hero of any Victorian novel, and *Punch* poked fun at him in its 'Rhodes Colossus' illustration in 1892.[21] In 1925 John Presland's *Dominion: A Novel of Cecil Rhodes and South Africa* and in 1932 Samuel Kemp's *Black Frontiers* were published, but in spite of the modest success of works the *Daily Mail* remarked that the inhabitants of Rhodes's home town were largely indifferent towards Rhodes and his legacy.[22]

As we have seen, the reputation of imperial heroes was never sacrosanct in the Victorian era and there was indeed plenty of criticism levelled at the actions of statesmen and generals from journalists and novelists. Perhaps it is the 'alternative' Victorian view of imperialists which has won out. The real heroes of the empire today are not the type of men conjured by G.A. Henty or Eva Hope in their novels and biographies.

The truly great men of the empire, in popular culture at least, are now people such as Gandhi who challenged colonial authority. But in some parts of the world even Gandhi is disliked. While the general public are most likely to be familiar with the movie version of Gandhi – a somewhat frail-looking older man played by Ben Kingsley who preaches tolerance and peace – the real Gandhi held some questionable views on race *in the early part of his life*, when he frequently referred to black people as *kaffirs*, a derogatory insult, and insisted that Indians were racially superior to them. So in December of 2018, after a long campaign with, of course, an obligatory Twitter hashtag, #GandhiMustFall, students at the University of Ghana succeeded in forcing their university's authorities to agree to remove Gandhi's statue.[23]

Nations will always look back to the past with nostalgia and gloss over the more unpleasant aspects of their history and actions of their famous historical figures. France and Italy, like Britain, have ongoing national debates about their past. So, how should we in the present view stories about the heroes of the British Empire? Perhaps, when we hear or read stories of such 'great men', we can adopt the same attitude as the eighteenth-century writer Henry Fielding (1707–54). With reference to the imperialists of Ancient Greece and Rome, he said that we should take all of the stories about the goodness, bravery, generosity, and altruism of historical military men with more than a pinch of salt and a healthy dose of downright cynicism:

In the histories of Alexander and Caesar we are frequently, and indeed impertinently, reminded of their benevolence and generosity, of their clemency and kindness. When the former had with fire and sword overrun a vast empire, had destroyed the lives of an immense number of innocent wretches, had scattered ruin and desolation like a whirlwind, we are told, as an example of his clemency, that he did not cut the throat of an old woman, and ravish her daughters, but was content with only undoing them. And when the mighty Caesar, with wonderful greatness of mind, had destroyed the liberties of his country, and with all the means of fraud and force had placed himself at the head of his equals, had corrupted and enslaved the greatest people whom the sun ever saw, we are reminded, as an evidence of his generosity, of his largesses to his followers and tools, by whose means he had accomplished his purpose, and by whose assistance he was to establish it. Now, who doth not see that such sneaking qualities as these are rather to be bewailed as imperfections than admired as ornaments in these great men?[24]

Notes

Preface: 'Checking Out Me History'

1. Walter Raleigh, *The Discovery of Guiana* (London, 1596), www.gutenberg. org (accessed 2 June 2019); John Agard, 'Checking Out Me History', genius. com (accessed 7 January 2019).
2. *An Act to make temporary provision for controlling the immigration into the United Kingdom of Commonwealth Citizens*, 10 & 11 Eliz. 2 c. 21 (London: HMSO, 1962); *An Act to amend sections 1 and 2 of the Commonwealth Immigrants Act 1962*, c. 9 (London: HMSO, 1968).
3. Carlyle, Thomas, *Sartor Resartus; Heroes; Chartism; Past and Present* (London: MacMillan [n.d.]), p. 186.
4. G.W. Hunt, *Macdermott's War Song* (London: Hopwood & Crew, 1877), p. 2.
5. Denham Harrison and W.T. Lytton, *Another Little Patch of Red* (New York: T.B. Harms, 1899), pp. 1–8.

Chapter 1: At Heaven's Command

1. The first European to reach Newfoundland was a Viking sailor named Leif Erikson (c. 970–c. 1020)
2. Charles Beazley, *John and Sebastien Cabot* (London: T.F. Unwin, 1898), p. xiv.
3. J.E. Wetherell, *Three Centuries of Canadian Story* (Toronto: Musson Book Company, 1928), p. 4.
4. John Dee, 'General and Rare Memorials', in *John Dee: Essential Readings*, ed. by Gerald Suster (Berkley, CA: North Atlantic Books, 2003), pp. 47–62 (p. 57).
5. Thomas Arne and James Thomson, 'Alfred: A Masque', in *Poetic Voices of the Eighteenth Century* (London: Charles Griffin, 1866), pp. 251–9 (p. 259).
6. Charles Johnson, *A General and True History of the Robberies and Murders of the Most Notorious Pyrates*, ed. by Arthur Heyward (London: Routledge, 1927), p. vii
7. Michael Drayton, 'Ode to the Virginian Voyage (1606)', in *The Poetry Foundation*, poetryfoundation.org (accessed 6 September 2018).
8. John Fletcher, 'Bonduca', in *The Works of Beaumont and Fletcher*, ed. by Henry Weber, 14 vols (Edinburgh: James Ballantyne, 1812), VI, pp. 58–9.

9. *Cobbett's Complete Collection of State Trials*, 33 vols (London, 1809–26), XX, pp. 79–82

10. William Cowper, 'The Task', in *Select Works of the British Poets*, ed. by Dr Aitkin, 10th edn (Philadelphia: Thomas Wardle, 1840), pp. 733–73 (p. 740).

11. 'Taxation in America', in *The Forget Me Not Songster* (New York: Nafis and Cornish [n.d.]), pp. 56–62 (p. 55).

12. 'Additional Instructions to Captain Cook', cited in Elizabeth Evatt, 'The Acquisition of Territory in Australia and New Zealand', in *Studies in the History of the Laws of Nations*, ed. by Charles Henry Alexandrowicz (The Hague: Martinus Nijhoff, 1970), pp. 16–45 (p. 20).

13. Earlier in time, between 1154 and 1215 under Kings Henry II, King Richard I, and King John, there was an empire – named the Angevin Empire by historians – whose centre was in England and comprised England, parts of Ireland and France.

14. Walter Scott, *Chronicles of the Canongate*, 2 vols (Edinburgh: Cadell, 1827), I, pp. 142–3.

15. Thomas Babington Macauley, *Minute on Education* (1835) cited in A.L. Harris, 'John Stuart Mill: Servant of the East India Company', in *John Stuart Mill: Critical Assessments*, ed. by John Cunningham Wood, 4 vols (London: Routledge, 1988), IV, pp. 207–25 (p. 217); Gibbs, pp. 102–3; Agnes Strickland, 'Candava; or, The Last Suttee', *The Home Circle*, 14 July 1849, 17–18.

16. W.J. Shepherd, *The Personal Narrative of the Outbreak and Massacre at Cawnpore* (London: R. Craven, 1879), p. 77.

17. Dickens was utterly reprehensible: a racist and anti-Semite, he was also a misogynist and treated his wife horribly.

18. Charles Dickens, 'To Angela Burdett Coutts', in *The Letters of Charles Dickens, 1856–1858*, ed. by Madeline House, Graham Storey and Kathleen Tillotson, 20 vols (Oxford: Clarendon Press, 1965–2002), VIII, p. 459.

19. Henry Morton Stanley, *Through the Dark Continent*, 2 vols (New York: Harper, 1878), p. 299.

Chapter 2: Wholesome and Amusing Literature

1. *Report from the Select Committee on the Copyright Acts* (1818) cited in Richard Altick, *The English Common Reader*, 3rd edn (Chicago: University of Chicago Press, 1963), p. 260. Book prices quoted for the works of Scott et al were taken from the information held in the British Fiction Database, 1800–29 (british-fiction.cf.ac.uk).

2. Edward P. Thompson, *The Making of the English Working Class*, 4th Edn (Pelican Books, 1972), pp. 342–3.

3. *Ibid.*, p. 275.

4. *A Dialogue between Farmer Trueman and his Son George about the Cannibals in India* (Liverpool: R. Tilling [n.d.]), p. 2.

5. *Robinson Crusoe* (Norwich: Lane and Walker [n.d.]), p. ii.
6. *Sorrowful lamentation of Benjamin Smith* (York: [n. pub.], 1816), p. i.
7. *The London 'Prentice Boy* ([n. pub.]: [n.p.] [n.d.]), p. i; *The Sorrowful Lamentation of the Unhappy Men in Bristol* (London: Printed by J. Phair, 76 Great Peter Street, Westminster, 1832), p. i; *Ten thousand miles away* (Preston: J. Harkness, 1840), p. i.
8. 'Black-Eyed Susan', in *The Forget Me Not Songster* (New York: Nafis and Cornish [n.d.]), pp. 131–2.
9. R.M. Ballantyne, *The Young Fur Traders* (London, 1856; repr. London: T. Nelson, 1901), p. 22.
10. 'The Works of G.P.R. James', *The Mirror Monthly Magazine*, November 1847, 323.
11. Charles Knight, *The Old Printer and the Modern Devil* (London: John Murray, 1854), p. 264, 284–8.
12. Mary Hammond, *Charles Dickens's Great Expectations: A Cultural Life, 1860–2012* (Abingdon: Routledge, 2015), p. 256.
13. Agnes Repplier, *Points of View* (New York: Houghton and Mifflin, 1893), p. 209
14. Charlotte M. Yonge, *What Books to Lend and What to Give* (London: [n.p.], [n.d.]), pp. 5–6.
15. 'The Literature of the Streets (1887)', cited in John Springhall, *Youth, Popular Culture and Moral Panics: Penny Gaffs to Gangsta-Rap, 1830–1996* (Basingstoke: MacMillan, 1998), p. 50.
16. *Blackie and Son's Books for Young People* (London: Blackie and Son [n.d.]), p. 19.
17. In other book advertisements, likewise, terms such as '12mo' mean duodecimo, indicating that a folio-size sheet of paper has been folded twelve times, similar in size to a modern paperback.
18. Jonathan Rose, *The Intellectual Life of the British Working Classes*, (Yale University Press, 2001), p. 191
19. Verena Pennefather, *Diary of Verena Vera Pennefather*, Bishopsgate Institute, GDP/51, Vol. 7 (1917).
20. Leslie Stephen, *Hours in the Library* (London: Smith, Elder & Co., 1878), p. 56
21. George Borrow cited in Susan Naramore Maher, 'Recasting Crusoe: Frederick Marryat, R.M. Ballantyne and the Nineteenth-Century Robinsonade', *Children's Literature Association Quarterly*, 13: 4 (1988), 169–75 (p. 69).
22. H. Rider Haggard, cited in Michael Arrighi, 'Telling Tales: Rider Haggard's Short Stories' (Unpublished MA thesis, University of Wollongong, 1991), p. 17.
23. H. Rider Haggard, *She: A History of Adventure* (London: Longmans, 1892), p. 174.

Chapter 3: Play Up! Play Up! And Play the Game!

1. Procopius cited in Saša Milojević, et al., *Youth and Hooliganism at Sporting Events* (Belgrade: Ministry of Education, 2013), pp. 21–2.
2. *Pierce Egan's Life in London and Sporting Guide*, 20 June 1824, 165.
3. Pierce Egan, *Boxiana; Sketches of Modern Pugilism*, 6 vols (London: Sherwood, Neeley and Jones, 1813–29), III, p. v.
4. Walter Scott, *Waverley; or, 'Tis Sixty Years Since* (Paris: Baudrey's European Library, 1839), pp. 161–2; Walter Scott, *The Letters of Walter Scott*, ed. by H.J.C. Grierson, 12 vols (London: Constable, 1933), IV, p. 80; Walter Scott, *The Surgeon's Daughter* (Edinburgh: Robert Cadell, 1833), p. 239.
5. Pierce Egan, *Boxiana; Sketches of Modern Pugilism*, I, p. 254.
6. *The Boys' Own Volume of Fact, Fiction, History, and Adventure* (London: S.O. Beeton, 1865), p. 447
7. Gilbert Jessop and J.B. Salmond, *The Book of School Sports* (London: Thomas Nelson [n.d.] c. 1920?), p. 10.
8. G.A. Henty, *At the Point of a Bayonet* (London: Blackie, 1902), p. 8.
9. He did occasionally branch out from writing fiction with such overtly imperialist themes by publishing novels set during the Napoleonic Wars (1793–1815), the Jacobite Rebellions of 1715 and 1745, and even the Peasants' Revolt of 1381.
10. G.A. Henty, *With Clive in India* (New York: Scribner and Welford [n.d.]), p. 9.
11. H.A. Guerber, *Myths and Legends of the Middle Ages* (London, 1896; repr. London: G. Harrap, 1909), p. 5. In a story retold by H.E. Marshall, young Beowulf has a swimming competition with Breca the Bronding, which Beowulf wins and afterwards receives a prize. This episode, which does appear in the original tale, was perfect material for Marshall to convey the imperial ideal of athleticism to younger readers by appropriating this tale from the distant past.
12. In the original Beowulf tale, which was retold by other Victorian writers, Beowulf returns home from his adventures in foreign lands and becomes ruler of his people, after which his name is 'known far and wide among all men as the symbol of courage and loyalty'. His illustrious career all started with his swimming/athletic prowess. *Ibid.*, pp. 16–17.
13. *Boys' Own Volume of Fact, Fiction, History, and Adventure*, p. 357.
14. H. Rider Haggard, *Eric Brighteyes*, (London: Longman, 1891), p. x.
15. Haggard, *Eric Brighteyes*, p. 11.
16. G.A. Henty, *Out with Garibaldi* (London: Blackie, 1901), pp. 64–6.
17. A.L.O.E., *The Robbers' Cave* (London, 1882), pp. 14–15: Italians were viewed as idle and devoid of that 'manly English spirit'.
18. Henty, *Out with Garibaldi*, p. 19.
19. Frederick Roberts, *Forty-One Years in India from Subaltern to Commander in Chief* (London: MacMillan, 1901), p. 542.

20. H. Rider Haggard, *King Solomon's Mines* (London, 1885), pp. 9–10.

21. Henty, *With Clive in India*, pp. 213–4.

22. Haggard, *King Solomon's Mines*, p. 194.

23. Thomas Arnold, '22 March 1828', in *The Life and Correspondence of Thomas Arnold*, ed. by Arthur Penryn Stanley (New York: Appleton, 1846), pp. 71–2.

24. Arnold, 'Letter of Inquiry for a Master', in Stanley, p. 91. Emphasis added.

25. Eva Hope, *The Life of General Gordon* (Edinburgh: Nimmo [n.d.]), p. 32.

26. *Murray's Magazine*, 2: 8 (1887), 145–64.

27. *Pictorial Sport and Adventure* (London: Frederick Warne [n.d.]), p. 184.

28. John S. Roberts, *The Life and Explorations of David Livingstone* (Boston: D. Lothrop, 1881), p. i.

29. *Young England, 1904–5* (London: Alexander and Shepheard, 1905), p. 468

30. *Ibid.*

31. *Heroes of the Empire* (London: John F. Shaw [n.d.]), p. 26.

32. Charles Knight's *Penny Magazine* featured several detailed illustrations of snakes, either in the midst of attacking prey or surrounding a charmer. Similarly, the cheap true crime magazines *The Illustrated Police News* and *The Police Gazette* loved a good deadly-snake story.

33. Two of G.W.M. Reynolds's penny bloods, *The Mysteries of London*, and *Wagner the Wehr-Wolf* (1846–47) depict fearsome encounters with snakes.

34. Bracebridge Hemyng, *Jack Harkaway After Schooldays* (London: E.J. Brett [n.d.]), p. 29: Jack finds a reticulated python on board the ship and is the only one 'manly' enough to kill it.

35. *Peter Parley's Annual: A Christmas and New Year's Present for Young People* (London [n.d.]), p. 119.

36. *The Boy's Own Paper*, 6 October 1894, 14.

37. *The Radleian* cited in J.A. Mangan, *The Games Ethic and Imperialism* (New York: Viking, 1986), p. 45.

38. *The Boys of the Empire*, 21 May 1888, 252.

39. G.A. Henty, *Tales of Daring and Danger* (London: Blackie, 1890), p. 133.

40. Robert Baden-Powell, *Sport in War* (London: William Heinemann, 1900), p. 3.

41. *Ibid.*, p. 7.

42. *Ibid.*, p. 8.

43. George W. Steevens, *Things Seen*, ed. by G.S. Street (Edinburgh: William Blackwood, 1869), p. 27.

44. *The New Sporting Magazine*, 2: 9 (1832), 157–64.

Chapter 4: For Right, For Freedom, For Fair Play!

1. Pierce Egan, *The Book of Sports and Mirror of Life* (London: T. Tegg, 1832), p. 334.

2. *Ibid.*, p. 335. Egan tells us that in March 1829, a wrestling match took place between James Copp and Francis Olver. The match seemed to be going

Olver's way until 'Olver seized Copp round the waist, and was gathering him in a fine position for the "home ting," but, having inadvertently grasped the handkerchief bound round Copp's body, he was compelled, by the rules of fair play, to relinquish his hold.'

3. *Ibid.*
5. *Ibid.*
6. 'Robin Hood and the Tanner', in *Robin Hood: A Collection of All the Ancient Poems, Songs, and Ballads*, ed. by Joseph Ritson, 2 vols (London: T. Egerton, 1795), II, pp. 30–7.
7. John Finnemore, *The Story of Robin Hood* (London, 1909; repr. London: A. & C. Black, 1935), p. x.
8. Ashley Somogyi, 'Young Knights of the Empire: The Impact of Chivalry on Literature and Propaganda of the First World War' (Unpublished PhD thesis, Durham University, 2018), p. 37.
9. Richard Hurd, *Letters on Chivalry and Romance*, ed. by Edith J. Morley (London: Henry Frowde, 1911), pp. 80–1.
10. Cited in Jeffrey Richards, *Films and British National Identity: From Dickens to Dad's Army* (Manchester University Press, 1994), p. 44.
11. *The Story of Ivanhoe for Children* (London: A.C. Black [n.d.]), p. vii.
12. Henry Newbolt, *The Book of the Happy Warrior* (London: Longmans, 1917), p. 279.
13. *Ibid.*
14. Baden-Powell, cited in Somogyi, p. 126.
15. Robert Baden-Powell, *Scouting for Boys* (London: H. Cox, 1908), p. 242.
16. F.S. Brereton, *With Roberts to Candahar* (London: Blackie [n.d.]), p. 10.
17. Hope, p. 356.
18. *Ibid.*
19. H. Major, *Up the Nile* (London: Wm Ibister Limited, 1887), pp. 127–8; F.M. Holmes, *Four Heroes of India* (London: S.W. Partridge [n.d.]), p. 37.
20. *The Boys of the Empire*, 13 February 1888, 222–3.
21. *The Boys of the Empire*, 4 June 1888, 284.
22. *Ibid.*
23. Ernest Foster, *Heroes of the Indian Empire* (London: Cassell, 1890), p. 72.
24. G.A. Henty, *By Sheer Pluck: A Tale of the Ashanti War* (London, 1884), cited in Jeffrey Richards, 'With Henty to Africa', in *Imperialism and Juvenile Literature*, ed. by Jeffrey Richards (Manchester University Press, 1989), pp. 72–106 (p. 102).
25. Rider Haggard, *She: A History of Adventure*, pp. 156–7.
26. *Ibid.*
27. *Ibid.*, p. 137.
28. *Ibid.*, p. 135.
29. *Ibid.*, p. 138.

Chapter 5: Over the Hills and Far Away

1. Robert Southey, *The Life of Nelson* (London: George Bell, 1888), p. 11.
2. *Ibid.*, p. 384.
3. *Ibid.*
4. George Farquhar, *The Recruiting Officer* (London: William Savage, 1706), II: 3.
5. Thomas D'Urfey, *Songs Compleat, Pleasant and Divertive*, 6 vols (London: J. Tonson, 1719), V, pp. 319–20.
6. Holmes, p. 92.
7. Samuel Johnson, 'Taxation No Tyranny', in *The Works of Samuel Johnson*, 16 vols (New York: Pafraets and Company, 1913), XIV, pp. 93–144.
8. 'Copy of petition from the Merchants, Traders, Manufacturers and other citizens of Bristol to George III' [c.1775]. Nottingham, Nottingham University Archives, Pw F 2717, 1r.
9. John Cartwright, *The Life and Correspondence of Major Cartwright*, ed. by F.D. Cartwright, 2 vols (London: Henry Colburn, 1826), I, pp.75–6.
10. Phebe Gibbs, *Hartly House, Calcutta*, ed. by Michael J. Franklin (Manchester University Press, 2019), p. 15.
11. *Norwich Mercury* cited in Kathleen Wilson, *The Sense of the People: Politics, Culture, and Imperialism in England, 1715–1785* (Cambridge University Press, 1998), p. 196.
12. John Dryden, 'King Arthur', in *The Works of John Dryden* (London: J. Tonson, 1735), pp. 362–420 (p. 363). Here we find, for example, the medieval King Arthur in the costume of a Roman centurion.
13. Charles Kingsley, *Westward Ho* (New York: Thomas E. Crowell [n.d.]), p. 12.
14. Robert Baden-Powell cited in Mangan, *The Games Ethic and Imperialism*, p. 48.
15. *The Empire Annual for Boys*, 14 (London: R.T.S. [n.d.]), pp. 35–9.
16. Alfred Noyes, *Drake: An English Epic. Books I–XII* (New York: Frederick A. Stokes, 1909), p. 280.
17. G.R. Gleig, *The Life of Arthur, Duke of Wellington* (London: Everyman, 1909), p. 64.
18. G.A. Henty, *With the Allies to Pekin* (New York: Scribner, 1903), p. 256.
19. Foster, p. 19.
20. *Ibid.*
21. *Ibid.*, p. 42.
22. Henty, *With Clive in India*, p. 25.
23. *Ibid.*, p. 377.
24. Roberts, p. 3.
25. *Chums*, 26 September 1900, 17.
26. R.M. Ballantyne, *The Young Fur Traders* (London, 1856; repr. London: T. Nelson, 1901), p. 26.

27. H.O. Arnold Foster, *Peril and Patriotism: True Tales of Heroic Deeds and Startling Adventures* (London: Cassell, 1906), p. 8.
28. David Campbell, *Victoria: Queen and Empress* (London: W.P. Nimmo, 1901), p. 268.
29. Hope, p. 4.
30. Hope, p. 320.
31. *Ibid.*
32. Arnold-Foster, p. 10.

Chapter 6: The Bad Boys of the Empire
  1. Rudyard Kipling, 'The White Man's Burden', in *Rudyard Kipling's Verse: Inclusive Edition, 1885–1918* (Garden City: Doubleday, 1922), ll. 1–8.
  2. Johnson, p. vii.
  3. Henry Fielding, *An Enquiry into the Causes of the Great Increase of Robbers* (Dublin: G. Faulkner, 1751), p. 3.
  4. The public panic over the perceived rise in crime did have a knock-on effect on some legislation. The legal response to this crime wave was the introduction of a bloody law code, when 200 offences became capital felonies.
  5. Johnson, p. vii.
  6. *Ibid.*, p. 134 and *The Female Smuggler* ([n. pub.]: [n.p.] [n.d.]), p. i. As is very common, there are no bibliographical details printed with this ballad. If people visit the Bodleian's Broadside Ballad online archive however, they are sure to find it.
  7. *Ibid.*, p. 334.
  8. *Ibid.*, p. 37.
  9. 'Captain Robert Kidd' in *The Forget Me Not Songster* (New York: Nafis and Cornish [n.d.]), pp. 28–33 (p. 29).
10. *Ibid.*, p. 32.
11. *The Pirate of the Isles* (Manchester: John Bebbington, c. 1850), p. i.
12. *The Pirate's Bride* (London: E. Hodges, c. 1865), p. i.
13. *The Boy's Comic Journal*, 22: 555 ([n.d.]), 226.
14. *Kit the Pirate; or, Life on the Ocean* (London: Newsagents Publishing Corp., 1865), p. 346.
15. Robert Louis Stevenson, cited in Oliver S. Buckton, 'Faithful to his Map: Profit and Desire in Robert Louis Stevenson's *Treasure Island*', *Journal of Stevenson Studies*, 1 (2004), 138–49 (p. 138).
16. Robert Louis Stevenson, *Treasure Island* (New York: Harper Brothers, 1915), p. i.
17. *Ibid.*, p. 32.
18. *Ibid.*, p. 68.
19. Grant Allen, 'Plain Words on the Woman Question', *Fortnightly Review*, 46 (1889), 454–5.

20. *The Boy's Halfpenny Journal*, 30 August 1879, 313–14 (p. 313).
21. Camden Palham, ed., *The Chronicles of Crime*, 2 vols (London: T. Miles, 1887), II, p. 472.
22. *Ibid.*, p. 473.
23. *Ibid.*
24. *Ibid.*
25. *Ibid.*
26. *Ibid.*
27. *Celebrated Trials and Remarkable Cases*, 6 vols (London: Knight and Lacey, 1825), IV, p. 307.
28. *The Criminal Recorder*, 4 vols (London, 1804–09; repr. London, 1815), I, p. 483.
29. *The New Newgate Calendar*, 7 November 1863, 41.
30. *Ibid.*, 42.
31. *The Boy's Halfpenny Journal*, 23 August 1879, 302.
32. *Ibid.*, 289–91 (p. 289).
33. Although it should be said that some of the magazines which published these stories did promote athleticism more generally. 'The King of the Outlaws' appeared in twelve instalments in the supposedly respectable periodical entitled *The Boys' Library* which in its masthead stated that it contained 'Cricket, Football, and Athletic Notes' as well as 'Serial and Complete Stories in Every Number'.
34. Bracebridge Hemyng, *Jack Harkaway's Schooldays* (London: Edwin J. Brett [n.d.]), p. 4.
35. Bracebridge Hemyng, *Jack Harkaway in the Transvaal* (London: Harkaway House, 1900), p. 55.
36. *Famous Crimes*, 8: 101 (n.d.), p. 37.
37. John Gay, *The Beggar's Opera* (London: J. Watts, 1729), p. 21: Captain Macheath counselled his fellow outlaws to 'act with conduct and discretion. A pistol is your last resort.'
38. While the novel was written anonymously, a note in the edition held in the Barry Ono Collection of Boys' Periodicals states that it was written by an Australian.
39. *Ned Kelly: The Australian Ironclad Bushranger* (London: Alfred J. Isaacs, 1881), p. 8.
40. *Ibid.*, p. 99.

Chapter 7: Desperadoes and Homicidal Madmen
1. Charles Cole, *A Poetical Address to His Grace the Duke of Wellington* (London: W. Strange, 1835), pp. 7–8.
2. *The Northern Star*, 21 May 1842, 1.
3. *The National Chartist Hymnbook* (Rochdale: National Chartist Foundation, c. 1845), p. 13.

4. Norbert J. Gossman, 'William Cuffay: London's Black Chartist', *Phylon*, 44: 1 (1983), 56–65 (p. 59).
5. 'A Rhyme for Canada', in *National Songs and Poetical Pieces*, ed. by Hugh Williams (London: H. Hetherington, 1839), p. 25.
6. 'Canadian Ode to Liberty', in Williams, p. 30.
7. Anon. [online] 'Revenge on India; to the Tune of The Soldier's Wife by D.J. Garrick, accessed 5 February 2020. Available at: http://ballads.bodleian. ox.ac.uk/
8. G.W.M. Reynolds, *Grace Darling: Heroine of the Fern Islands. A Tale Founded Upon Facts* (London: G. Henderson, 1839), p. vi.
9. *Ibid*.
10. *Reynolds's Miscellany*, 6 February 1869, 126.
11. *Reynolds's Newspaper*, 3 November 1850, 1.
12. G.W.M. Reynolds, cited in Antony Taylor, 'Some little or contemptible war upon her hands: *Reynolds's Newspaper* and empire', in *G.W.M. Reynolds: Nineteenth-Century Fiction, Politics and the Press*, ed. by Anne Humpherys and Louis James (Aldershot, Ashgate, 2008), pp. 99–119.
13. *The Chartist Circular*, 21 December 1839, 52.
14. *The Chartist Circular*, 28 December 28, 1839, 56.
15. *Reynolds's Newspaper*, 29 August 1897, 2.
16. *The Northern Star*, 28 June 1851, 4.
17. *Ibid*.
18. Pierce Egan, *Paul Jones the Privateer* (London: F. Hextall, 1842), pp. 540–41. Egan's novel was not the first time that Jones's story had been adapted for British audiences however, for the famous Victorian playwright Thomas Dibdin had written *Paul Jones* which premiered at Sadler's Wells Theatre in 1827, and the publisher John Dicks reprinted a penny edition of the script text for families to perform at home.
19. Pierce Egan, *Clifton Grey* (London: W.S. Johnson, 1856), p. ii.
20. G.W.M. Reynolds, *The Mysteries of London*, 2 vols (London: G. Vickers, 1848), I, p. 2.
21. *Ibid*, II, p. 194.
22. *Reynolds's Newspaper*, 3 November 1850, 1.
23. G.W.M. Reynolds, *The Soldier's Wife* (London: J. Dicks, 1866), p. 10.
24. 'The Soldier's Catechism', in *Curiosities of Street Literature*, ed. by Charles Hindley, 2 vols (London: Reeves and Turner, 1871), I, p. 89.
25. *Reynolds's Newspaper*, 8 September 1850, 1.
26. *Reynolds's Newspaper*, 30 March 1851, 1.
27. 'Literary Notices', *Cleave's Penny Gazette*, 18 August 1838, 2. This is the only contemporary literary notice to draw attention to this obscure work by Reynolds. I have not seen a copy myself, and it is not listed in the bibliographies of any of the scholarly works on Reynolds's life and works.
28. G.W.M. Reynolds, *Pickwick Abroad* (London, 1838; repr. London: Willoughby [n.d.]), p. 49.

29. 'The Tri-Coloured Flag', in Williams, p. 34.
30. *Northern Star*, 25 March 1848, 3. Even the Chartists were, relatively speaking, comfortable with industrial capitalism and imperialism. A poem reprinted in this issue, for example, criticised 'Empire based upon a wrong' but never called for an end to imperialism.
31. *Punch*, 21 September 1878, 178.
32. *The Radical*, 8 January 1881, 1.
33. Brereton, p. 352.
34. Karl Marx and Friedrich Engels, *The Communist Manifesto* (London: Verso, 2012), p. 1.
35. *Commonweal*, February (1885), 2–3.
36. *Commonweal*, 1: 9 (1885), 86–87 (p. 86).
37. *The Northern Star*, 1 January 1848, cited in Mike Sanders, *The Poetry of Chartism* (Cambridge University Press, 2009), p. 173. Earlier in the Chartist period, *The Northern Star* had given qualified support to Irish nationalism, but the paper's editorial stance was, on the whole, uncomfortable with the 'nationality humbug'.
38. *Ibid.*, 87.
39. William Morris, *News from Nowhere* (London: Kelmscott, 1892), p. 2.
40. *Ibid.*, pp. 1–2.
41. *Ibid.*, pp. 12–13.
42. *Ibid.*, pp. 136–8.
43. *The Social Democrat*, 4 (1897), 99–103 (p. 100).
44. Annie Besant cited in 'Reviews of Books', *Reynolds's Newspaper*, 26 January 1879, 6.
45. *Ibid.*
46. *Ibid.*
47. *Reynolds's Newspaper*, 3 June 1894, 2.
48. R.M. MacDonald, *Labour and the Empire* (London, 1907), p. 36, 112.
49. Robert Blatchford cited in Paul Ward, *Red Flag and Union Jack: Englishness, Patriotism, and the British Left, 1881–1924* (Woodbridge: Boydell, 1998), p. 60 and Robert Blatchford, cited in James Connolly, 'Imperialism and Socialism (1899)', in *James Connolly: Selected Political Writings*, ed. by Owen Dudley Edwards and Bernard Ransom (London: Cape, 1973), pp. 226–7.
50. Escott Lynn, 'A Daughter of the Veldt', *"My Queen" Library*, 237 (n.d.), 3.
51. Connolly, p. 227.

Chapter 8: Heroes No More

1. Matthew Prior, 'Solomon', in *The Poetical Works of Matthew Prior*, ed. by Thomas Park, 3 vols (London: Stanhope Press, 1807), III, pp. 29–40; *Reynolds's Newspaper*, 22 July 1900, 1.
2. William Morris, 'To Eirikr Magnusson', in *The Collected Letters of William Morris, 1885–88*, ed. by Norman Kelvin, 5 vols (Princeton, NJ: Princeton

University Press, 1984–87), III, p. 785. Rider Haggard was actually good friends with William Morris, and in some of Rider Haggard's later works, Morris's influence can be felt.

3. H. Rider Haggard, *Allan Quatermain*, (London: Longman, 1894), pp. 4–5.
4. H. Rider Haggard, *Ayesha: The Return of She* (London, 1905), pp. 322–3.
5. Rider Haggard cited in Peter Berresford Ellis, *H. Rider Haggard: A Voice from the Infinite* (London: Routledge, 1978), p. 148.
6. I offer as two examples from the Mass Observation archive the following (though there are other instances of these novels being read as well): KB3/2/40, 'Eustace Road', Mass Observation Reading Habits, 1937–47; 20/2/D, '17 Years. Girl. Boarding School', Mass Observation Reading Habits, 1937–47.
7. C.S. Forester, *Beat to Quarters* (Boston: Little, Brown and Company, 1937), p. 20.
8. *The Fortnightly Review*, 94: 559 (1913), 12–28.
9. Lytton Strachey, *Eminent Victorians* (London: Chatto and Windus, 1932), p. 186. Strachey criticised Arnold for the fact that his reforms of Rugby were largely meaningless. Cardinal Manning, Victorian England's famous convert to Roman Catholicism, was nothing but a religious hypocrite.
10. *Ibid.*, p. 115.
11. *Ibid.*, p. 161.
12. *Ibid.*, pp. 222–3.
13. Edmund Wilson, cited in Lytton Strachey, *Eminent Victorians* (London: Modern Library, 1999), p. 1.
14. E.M. Forster, *A Passage to India*, ed. by Christel R. Devadawson (London: Longman, 1969), p. 41.
15. Richard Nixon, cited in László Borhi, 'Containment, Rollback, Liberation or Inaction? The United States and Hungary in the 1950s', *Journal of Cold War Studies*, 1: 3 (1999), 67–108.
16. George MacDonald Fraser, *Flashman's Lady* (London: Harper Collins, 1993), p. 13.
17. *Guardian*, 4 March 2015, theguardian.com (accessed 17 January 2019).
18. *The Telegraph*, 23 May 2002, telegraph.co.uk (accessed 30 October 2018).
19. *Reynolds's Newspaper*, 25 June 1899, 5.
20. *Reynolds's Newspaper*, 1 April 1900, 4.
21. *Punch*, 10 December 1892, p. 266.
22. *Daily Mail*, 28 August 1935, 8.
23. *BBC News*, 13 December 2018, bbc.co.uk (accessed 6 January 2019).
24. Henry Fielding, 'The Life of Mr Jonathan Wild the Great', in *The Works of Henry Fielding: Complete in One Volume*, ed. by Thomas Roscoe (London: Henry Washbourne, 1841), p. 540.

Select Bibliography

All references to relevant primary sources have been listed in the notes section. The following is a list of secondary sources which have informed my research. Should anyone wish to see a full bibliography, they are welcome to email me: Stephen. basdeo@outlook.com. *Alternatively, a full list of all secondary sources I consulted has also been uploaded to my academia.edu profile.*

Altick, Richard, *The English Common Reader: A Social History of the Mass Reading Public, 1800–1900*, 3rd edn (Chicago: The University of Chicago Press, 1963)

Armstrong, Christopher S., 'The Lessons of Sports: Class Socialization in British and American Boarding Schools', *Sociology of Sport Journal*, 1: 4 (1984), 314–31

Atkinson, Harriet. *The Festival of Britain: A land and its People* (London: IB Tauris, 2012)

Banivanua-Mar, Tracey, 'Cannibalism and Colonialism: Charting Colonies and Frontiers in Nineteenth-Century Fiji', *Comparative Studies in Society and History*, 52: 2 (2010), 255–81

Basdeo, Stephen, 'Radical Medievalism: Pierce Egan the Younger's Robin Hood, Wat Tyler, and Adam Bell', in *Imagining the Victorians*, ed. by Stephen Basdeo and Lauren Padgett, Leeds Working Papers in Victorian Studies, 15 (Leeds: Leeds Centre for Victorian Studies, 2016), pp. 48–65

——, *Robin Hood: The Life and Legend of an Outlaw* (Barnsley: Pen and Sword, 2018)

Belk, Patrick Scott, *Empires of Print: Adventure Fiction in the Magazines, 1899–1919* (Abingdon: Routledge, 2017)

Biber, Katherine, 'The Emperor's New Clones: Indiana Jones and Masculinity in Reagan's America', *Australasian Journal of American Studies*, 14: 2 (1995), 67–86

Bowen, H.V., *War and British Society 1688–1815* (Cambridge University Press, 1998)

Bridge, Carl and Kent Fedorovich, 'Mapping the British World', in *The New Imperial Histories Reader*, ed. by Stephen Howe (Abingdon: Routledge, 2010), pp. 147–59

Carver, Stephen, *The 19th-Century Underworld: Crime, Controversy and Corruption* (Barnsley: Pen and Sword, 2018)

Clendinning, Anne, 'On the British Empire Exhibition, 1924–25', branchcollective.org (accessed 29 October 2018)

Collins, Tony, *Sport in Capitalist Society: A Short History* (Abingdon: Routledge, 2013)

Crook, Paul, 'Social Darwinism and British "new imperialism": Second thoughts', *The European Legacy: Toward New Paradigms*, 3: 1 (1998), 1–16

De Groot, J., 'Metropolitan desires and colonial connections', in *At Home with the Empire*, ed. by Catherine Hall and Sonya Rose (Cambridge University Press, 2006)

Ellis, H., 'Thomas Arnold, Christian Manliness and the Problem of Boyhood', *Journal of Victorian Culture*, 19: 4 (2014), 425–41

Faller, Lincoln B., *Turned to Account: The Forms and Functions of Criminal Biography in Late-Seventeenth and Early Eighteenth-Century England* (Cambridge University Press, 1987)

Ferguson, Niall, *Empire: How Britain Made the Modern World* (London: Allen Lane, 2003)

Frost, Ginger S., *Victorian Childhoods* (Westport, CT: Praeger, 2009)

Godfrey, Esther, 'Victorian Cougar: H. Rider Haggard's *She*, Ageing, and Sexual Selection in Marriage', *Victorian Network*, 4: 2 (2012), 72–86

Gossman, Norbert J., 'William Cuffay: London's Black Chartist', *Phylon*, 44: 1 (1983), 56–65

Hall, Catherine and Sonya Rose, eds., *At Home with the Empire* (Cambridge University Press, 2006)

Hall, Donald, ed., *Muscular Christianity: Embodying the Victorian Age* (Cambridge University Press, 1994)

Heinonen, Alayna, 'A Tonic to the Empire? The 1951 Festival of Britain and the Empire-Commonwealth', *Britain and the World*, 8: 1 (2015), 76–99

Heywood, Ian, *The Revolution in Popular Literature: Print, Politics, and the People* (Cambridge University Press, 2004)

Hobsbawm, *Bandits*, rev. ed. (London: Abacus, 2003)

Hoffenberg, P., *An Empire on Display* (Berkeley, CA: University of California Press, 2001)

Holt, J., *Public School Literature, Civic Education and the Politics of Male Adolescence* (Farnham: Ashgate, 2008)

Howe, Stephen, *Empire: A Very Short Introduction* (Oxford University Press, 2002)

——, ed., *The New Imperial Histories Reader* (Abingdon: Routledge, 2010)

Howsam, Leslie, ed., *The Cambridge Companion to the History of the Book* (Cambridge University Press, 2015)

Humpherys, Anne and Louis James, eds., *G.W.M. Reynolds Nineteenth-Century Fiction, Politics, and the Press* (Farnham: Ashgate, 2008)

James, Lawrence, *The Rise and Fall of the British Empire* (London: Abacus, 1994)

Jowitt, Claire, 'Colonialism, Politics, and Romanization in John Fletcher's *Bonduca*', *SEL: Studies in English Literature, 1500–1900*, 43: 2 (2003), 475–94

Katz, Wendy R., 'Stevenson, Conrad and the Idea of the Gentleman: Long John Silver and Gentleman Brown', *Journal of Stevenson Studies*, 3 (2006), 51–69

Kingstone, Helen, *Victorian Narratives of the Recent Past: Memory, History, Fiction* (Basingstoke: Palgrave, 2017)

Kirkpatrick, Robert, *From the Penny Dreadful to the Ha'penny Dreadfuller: A Bibliographical History of the British Boys' Periodical 1762–1950* (London: British Library Publishing, 2013)

——, *Wild Boys in the Dock: Victorian Juvenile Literature and Juvenile Crime*, Occasional Papers XI (London: Children's Books History Society, 2013)

Knight, Stephen, *Robin Hood: A Mythic Biography* (Ithaca: Cornell University Press, 2003)

Little, Becky, 'Bond – James Bond – Was Created to Mourn the British Empire', *History*, 2 August 2017, history.com (accessed 22 February 2019)

MacKenzie, John, 'Empire and Metropolitan Cultures', in *The Oxford History of the British Empire: The Nineteenth*-Century, ed. by A. Porter, 5 vols (Oxford University Press, 1998–99), 3: 270–93

——, ed., *Imperialism and Popular Culture* (Manchester University Press, 1986)

——, *Propaganda and Empire: The Manipulation of British Public Opinion, 1880–1960* (Manchester University Press, 1984)

Mangan, J.A., ed., *Benefits Bestowed? Education and British Imperialism*, rev. ed. (Abingdon: Routledge, 2012)

——, *A Sport-Loving Society: Victorian and Edwardian Middle-Class England at Play* (Abingdon: Routledge, 2006)

——, *The Games Ethic and Imperialism: Aspects of the Diffusion of an Ideal* (London: Viking, 1986)

——, *Athleticism in the Victorian and Edwardian Public School: The Emergence and Consolidation of an Educational Ideology* (Cambridge University Press, 1981)

Marriott, John, *The Other Empire: Metropolis, India and Progress in the Colonial Imagination* (Manchester University Press, 2003)

May, Trevor, *The Victorian Public School* (Oxford: Shire, 2011)

Michals, Teresa, *Books for Adults, Books for Children: Age and the Novel from Defoe to James* (Cambridge University Press, 2014)

Mitchell, Rosemary, *Picturing the Past: English History in Text and Image, 1830–1870* (Oxford University Press, 2000)

Mosley, Stephen, *The Environment in World History* (Abingdon: Routledge, 2010)

Murphy, Patricia, 'The Gendering of History in "She"', *Studies in English Literature, 1500–1900*, 39: 4, The Nineteenth Century (1999), 747–72

Noimann, Chamutal. 'He a Cripple and I a Boy: The Pirate and the Gentleman in Robert Louis Stevenson's Treasure Island', *The Washington & Jefferson College Review*, 58 (2012), 55–71

Pakenham, Thomas, *The Scramble for Africa* (London: Abacus, 1990)

Parker, Matthew, *Goldeneye – Where Bond Was Born: Ian Fleming's Jamaica* (London: Pegasus, 2015)

Parry, Glyn, 'John Dee and the Elizabethan British Empire in its European Context', *The Historical Journal*, 49: 3 (2006), 643–75

Pearson, David, *Books as History*, rev. ed. (London: British Library, 2012)

Poklad, Josh, 'From Focus to Fragmentation: Commodity Spectacle and Political Agency, 1851–1914' (Unpublished PhD thesis, University of Leeds, 2018)

Porter, A., ed., *The Oxford History of the British Empire*, 5 vols (Oxford University Press, 1998–99)

Porter, B., *The Absent-Minded Imperialists* (Oxford University Press, 2004)

Reynolds, Matthew, *The Realms of Verse 1830–1870: English Poetry in a Time of Nation-Building* (Oxford University Press, 2001)

Richards, Jeffrey, *Films and British National Identity: From Dickens to Dad's Army* (Manchester University Press, 1994)

——, ed., *Imperialism and Juvenile Literature* (Manchester University Press, 1989)

Rose, Jonathan, *The Intellectual Life of the British Working Classes* (Yale University Press, 2001)

Said, Edward, *Orientalism*, 3rd edn (London: Penguin, 2003)

——, *Culture and Imperialism* (New York: Vintage, 1994)

Sanders, Mike, *The Poetry of Chartism* (Cambridge University Press, 2009)

Searle, G.R., *A New England?* (Oxford University Press, 2004)

Shep, Sydney, 'Books in Global Perspective', in *The Cambridge Companion to the History of the Book*, ed. by Leslie Howsam (Cambridge University Press, 2015), pp. 53–72

Snowdon, David, *Writing the Prizefight: Pierce Egan's Boxiana World* (Bern: Peter Lang, 2013)

Summerfield, Penny, 'Patriotism and Empire: Music Hall Entertainment 1870–1914', in *Imperialism and Popular Culture*, ed. by John MacKenzie (Manchester University Press, 1986)

Taylor, Antony, "Some Little or Contemptible War upon her Hands": *Reynolds's Newspaper* and Empire', in *G.W.M. Reynolds Nineteenth-Century Fiction, Politics, and the Press*, ed. by Anne Humpherys and Louis James (Farnham: Ashgate, 2008), pp. 99–122

Thompson, Andrew, *The Empire Strikes Back?* (London: Pearson, 2005)

——, 'The Language of Imperialism and the Meanings of Empire', in *The New Imperial Histories Reader*, ed. by Stephen Howe (Abingdon: Routledge, 2010), pp. 306–22

Tickell, Alex, *Terrorism, Insurgency and Indian-English Literature, 1830–1947* (Abingdon: Routledge, 2013)

Tosh, John, *A Man's Place: Masculinity and the Middle-Class Home in Victorian England* (Yale University Press, 1999)

Vargo, Gregory, "Outworks of the Citadel of Corruption": The Chartist Press Reports the Empire', *Victorian Studies*, 54: 2 (2012), 227–53

Varisco, Daniel Martin, *Reading Orientalism: Said and the Unsaid* (Seattle, WA: University of Washington Press, 2008)

Wallbank, M.V., 'Eighteenth-Century Public Schools and the Education of the Governing Elite', *Journal of the History of Education Society*, 8: 1 (1979), 1–19

Ward, Paul, *Red Flag and Union Jack: Englishness, Patriotism, and the British Left, 1881–1924* (Woodbridge: Boydell, 1998)

Warraq, Ibn, *Defending the West: A Critique of Edward Said's Orientalism* (Amherst, NY: Prometheus, 2007)

Williams, Eric, *Capitalism and Slavery* (Chapel Hill, NC: University of North Carolina Press, 1944)

W. Lee, C. J. W., 'Christian Manliness and National Identity: The Problematic Construction of a Racially "Pure" Nation', in *Muscular Christianity: Embodying the Victorian Age*, ed. by Donald Hall (Cambridge University Press, 1994), pp. 66–90

Index